This Book Is Dedicated to Our Heavenly Father!
I give him all of the glory and credit for my talents and gifts. I am honored to be used as an instrument for the Kingdom of God.
While I was writing this book, God healed my heart and delivered me from the wounds of my past. Through Jesus Christ, I am more than an OVERCOMER and I am living proof of it today. I claim this book will capture your heart and you will decide not to just overcome but live life as more than an
OVERCOMER!

Book Reviews

"While reading Megan's story, it became clear the transformation God has performed in her life. I met Megan through my husband and she has become a very special part of my life. When I look at her, I see myself as a young lady. Megan and I have shared the dark secret of abuse and overcoming it through our precious savior, Jesus Christ.

Everything she writes is a true reflection of Megan. She carries the beautiful fruit of the spirit and an exciting love of God. She is gentle, loving, and a precious woman of God. This book truly reflects her faith, love, and willingness to share the love of God. I praise her for her boldness to release this dark, secret so that others can overcome as we have.

I speak love and blessing over Kyle and Megan. I know God has great and exciting plans for both of you!"

– Nadine A. Williams, fellow worshipper of Christ and Proverbs 31 woman

"I'm the kind of reader that often jumps around in a book, eager to seek the pages that jump out at me. Instead, reading this book helped me to go back and forth so I didn't miss anything. Her story is captivating. She will lead you to that place of victory that God has for every person on this planet whether you have a relationship with Jesus yet or not.

This book helped me to not only understand others who go through so much to gain a testimony of victory, but I believe for those that are in places of defeat in any area of their life that can read Megan's journey and quickly discover that God has a place for them that is so special in this life that he opens doors NO ONE can shut! As the reader is gaining perspective of what God can do for one person, he can do for you also. She shares the lies of the enemy that held her captive for so long and many of the same lies the enemy uses on us all to keep us in a place where he can creep in to kill, steal, and destroy you and your life. Then, by the end of the book, she is calling you to a place of stepping forward in your life, into a place of worship and praise, and being in a secret place in his presence where you are treasured by your creator and cannot be moved.

My favorite parts are how she begins to recognize who God is sending in her life to influence her and lead her to her promised land. I also love how she begins to realize her husband's special place in her life. For me, she has become a part of my life's calling that I didn't truly know I had and she has shown me that for each of us, we have a powerful story and gifting and when we are in the purpose of God has for us, he'll use us mightily person by person to help others along and to become More than an Overcomer. I declare that each person will walk in a victorious, abundant life of Overcoming whatever we are each faced with on a daily basis, in Jesus Name! Now is the time. It's your season. Step forward."

- Leah Coleman, radical faith chick, wife, lover of God and people

"Having a similar battle to fight in my childhood; I was comforted and encouraged by Megan's victorious testimony of God's unfailing love. Her love story with Jesus at the center has propelled my spirit with greater faith, hope, and love. I'm also reminded how high Jesus has elevated me far above the battlefield of my past. Be filled with love and compassion for Jesus as you experience the depths of his love for you. Invite Jesus into your heart and surrender all unforgiveness and in him you will find life abounding with overflowing freedom and jumping joy!"

Through Jesus, we are all "More than an Overcomer." Megan, thank you for ministering the love of Jesus by being obedient and allowing him to flow through you straight into my heart. I love you my precious sister in Christ. Be his love and light to many as we move further into his glory.

- Bridget Grindstaff, evangelist, wife, and sister in Christ Jesus

Contents

†

"For with God nothing shall be impossible."
Luke 1:37

My testimony was written when I was entering the beginning of my healing process with the Lord. My healing was done supernaturally through the blood of the lamb. I give God all of the glory for my healing and for the woman I am today. Today, I am set free and healed from the hurts, pain, and wounds of my past. Now, listen to my testimony and learn how our amazing God performed a miraculous work through my life.

True Freedom: Fly and Soar Into What God has called you To Be

✝

"But those who trust in the Lord will find new strength. They will soar on wings like eagles. They will run and not grow weary. They will walk and not faint."

Isaiah 40:31

I have held this secret to long. It has been with me for the most of my life. It is time to share this secret with others. I refuse and cannot hold this in no longer. I need to release this secret that follows me everywhere I go. No matter how far I run it is still there. I try to cover up the evidence of this secret, but it keeps being revealed to me. I try to act like it is not there, but it keeps speaking to me. This secret that I am about to share with you is not just any secret, but a testimony of how real God is and he can change anybody. God changed me, he can change anybody, and I mean anybody.

God created me in my mother's womb. In Jeremiah 1:5, "Before I formed you in the belly I knew you; and before you came forth out of the womb I sanctified you, and I ordained you a prophet unto the nations." He created and chose me before I was even

5

thought of. In Genesis 1:27, "So God created man in his own image, in the image of God created he him; male and female created he them." God shaped and molded me into his very image. He had it already planned out. God has a divine purpose and master plan for my life. It is so amazing that no matter what happens, he is always there. He knows what is going to happen before it even happens. God is never surprised. I truly believe he turns around everything for our good. In Romans 8:28, "And we know that all things work together for good to them that love God, to them who are the called according to his purpose." Only good gifts come from our Heavenly Father. He even inspired my mom to pick my full name. I hope she realizes that God's hand is at work in my life includes the name given to me. The meaning of Megan and Margaret is mighty and pearl. In Matthew 13:45-46, "Again, the kingdom of heaven is like unto a merchant man, seeking goodly pearls: Who, when he had found one pearl of great price, went and sold all that he had, and bought it." God specifically handcrafted my name. Pearl is one of God's precious jewels. In Malachi 3:17, "And they shall be mine, says the Lord of hosts, in that day when I publicly recognize and openly declare them to be my jewels (My special possessions, my peculiar treasure). And I will spare them, as a man spares his own son who serves him." What is truly special and precious like pearl encounters a process of irritation and transformation before it becomes this amazing jewel that is polished with beauty and pureness. Just like how a pearl goes through a process, our life is a process to prepare us for the explosive blessings that our Heavenly Father has in store for us. God uses our life to help others and for him to be glorified. I can say that God has used my life to help so many people along the way including my family. My family has seen the

6

complete transformation that God has performed in my life and they hunger for God to do the same. Several of my family members have accepted and submitted their lives to Jesus Christ. My family has watched and recognized what God has done in my life. It is not only the words we use, but the way we live our lives that can impact the people around us. I truly believe that God created and called me into this world to make a positive difference in the lives of others and to help people to find their true identity in Christ Jesus.

Furthermore, when I was in my mother's womb and even after I was born, Satan attempted to destroy and hinder me from fulfilling God's plan for my life, but God is more powerful and greater than anyone and anything. God has faithfully continued to protect and guard me with his mighty angels. My birth was not an accident but a Miracle from God. My earthly Dad, David Thomas reminds with these loving and kind words, "Megan, you were the first MIRACLE baby." My Dad (stroke survivor and an amazing Dad who God could only change) said, "You came out of your mother's womb purple and not breathing. The doctors said you were not going to make it but you did. We found out if you were born naturally, then you would have been hung." As I grew older, my Dad shared with me that I was on a breathing machine for 24 months because of the difficulty I had breathing on my own. My Dad told me that he remembers the constant nights of the machine going off because my heart stopped. My parents would have to wake up in the middle of the night and shake me to start breathing again or call the paramedics. My Dad said I had constant ear infections and I was allergic to tap water.

Satan attempted to use whatever he could to hinder me from being alive today, but God had a different plan. It is amazing to know my whole body was placed in the living hands of our Heavenly Father. In Psalm 139:13-14, "You have covered me in my mother's womb. I will praise you; for I am fearfully and wonderfully made: marvelous are thy works; and that my soul knows right well." He protected and secured my pathway to be here today. God turned around what Satan meant for harm to something good and extraordinary.

At the age of 4, my parents separated. When they were together, all I remember is the constant arguing, fighting, and yelling. When my parents separated, I remember waking up to my 3 year old brother crying at the top of lungs for our mom. I remember searching for her throughout the house and never was able to find her. During those times, I recall laying there with my brother and rocking him to sleep. Later in my life, I found out that she was at bars drinking and searching for men. When my mom was upset she would yell and let out all of her frustration towards us, children. She had constant mood swings and her emotions would cause her to get angry and violent. My reaction to her was to run, hide, and cry out for help. My whole life I was running from something; people, things, circumstances, situations, or pressure, but now I run to Jesus. Before I knew Christ, I was living in anger, low self-esteem, loneliness, depression, fear, doubt, physical, mental, and verbal abuse. I was rejected by my family and people I thought were friends, but really weren't my friends. I was living in a house that didn't say, "I love you" or act in love. Instead of the acceptance of love, there was hatred, envy, fear, worry, and doubt. I was told, "You are unworthy. Who do you think you are? You are nobody. You are ugly. Who could ever love you? You don't even exist. Nobody loves you. You were adopted and you don't belong to this family. You will never mount up to anything. You disgust me. You make me sick," by the people that I thought loved and cared for me. When I accepted Jesus as my Lord and Savior, I learned that those words were lies from Satan. The Devil is Father of Lies. I remember from the age of 4 to 18, Satan would put thoughts in my mind of taking my life, so that I wouldn't have to run anymore and it would take all of the pain away. Again, that is a lie from Satan. I remember the thoughts of you don't exist or no one cares or loves you, so why are you still here. Of course, that was a lie from the Devil to tempt me into a stage of self-pity and depression.

My life was heading into the direction of no sense of purpose and meaning. I felt sacred and alone. When I sensed that my brothers, sister, and I were in danger, I would shield and cover them from harm. When my mom's boyfriend would come into the house with anger, resentment, fear, and violence, I would immediately grab my brothers and sister and hide them. I made up my mind that he would have to come through me to reach them. From age 4 to 16, I experienced beatings, slapping across the face, spitting in my face, my hair being pulled out, name calling, my arms being twisted, objects thrown at me, and threats. Over the course of 12 years, my mom's boyfriend continued to release his anger and fear onto us, children. Also, I watched my brother pick up and carry on with his bad habits. I pray and claim that God is changing his heart, right now.

Furthermore, I sensed my life was caving in and that there was no way out. I felt like I was living in a prison and all I needed was the key to get out. The prison was in my mind and I was stuck in the fear, worry, doubt, and loneliness mentality. From childhood to teenage years, I stayed in my room or waited until my mom's boyfriend left the house for an escape. I was afraid and sacred that something bad was going to occur. I never really had a childhood. I spent my weekends and summers watching my brothers and sister and cleaning the dirt off of the walls and floors. The house we lived in wore the traces of the filth that was in our lives. My brothers, sister, and I walked around with sickness, hunger, fear, and confusion. Satan is the author of confusion and fear. In 1 Timothy 1:7, "For God has not given us the spirit of fear; but of power, and of love, and of a sound mind." I always have had a heart of compassion for others and I never agreed with the way we lived. My heart reached out for my brothers and sister with love and service. I always made sure they were fed and clothed before my own needs. My desire was always to help, nurture, and care for them, but Jesus showed me that I was to cast all of the cares unto him. If my brother or sister were upset or anger, I would act on what they felt.

During my childhood, I remember nights of empty stomachs and heartaches. I would wake up in the morning with excitement to eat a meal at school and to receive an education, but I faced bullying and name-calling at school. I walked around with a fake smile to try to hide and cover the wounds of hurt. People that I thought were friends turned on me and started gossiping about pieces of my secret. When I shared with so-called friends about my secret, they promised and swore to never share it with anybody, but later on, people at school found out. When other people found out, they were angry, frustrated, and condemned me for not leaving or escaping the horrific lifestyle, but I felt obligated to protect and secure my brothers and sister. It troubled me to leave without them, but eventually made the step to walk away from my past.

At the age of 15, I started dating my daycare crush, who is now my husband. I have to stop and say to the love of my life, "I thank God everyday for you, honey. I honor and respect you, Kyle as my husband and best friend. I love you and thank you for not giving up on me. Thank you for not walking away from me when you had the chance. I thank God for giving me you! You are a gift from heaven. You have encouraged, loved, and helped me through my healing process. I am truly grateful for you and what God is doing through us to bless others. God has put us together for a reason. I knew in my heart at daycare you were the one. I prayed if you were the one that God would bring you back into my life. God is so faithful. Thank you for walking in love and forgiveness. I love you sweetheart and I will never forget that God is the reason for our strong, healthy marriage. I love you for who you are and who you have become in Christ. I give God all of the glory for you! You are an "Angel.""

Ladies, if you have a good man or husband, don't take him for granted. Honor and obey your husband. Avoid strife and always run to the word of God for answers. God's word is the only answer to your situation or circumstance and it is a powerful weapon. I thank God for giving me my husband. God knows we need each other. When my husband and I get together, we are powerful prayer warriors and no Devil in Hell can come between us. We refuse to give up and we know God has a BIG calling on our lives. It is God's will for us to be together. It takes three, you, your spouse, and God – the center of your marriage. God's word has helped Kyle and I to experience a victorious and successful life together. We continue to seek God daily for his plan and purpose for our life. Kyle and I thank God for our healing and his unconditional love towards us.

Our friends see who we are today in Christ Jesus. They look at Kyle and I as a man and woman of God. My women friends recognize me as a woman filled of God's beauty, joy, love, faith, peace, confidence, boldness, and courage. I am a woman with a powerful testimony to uplift and inspire women all around the world. I am who I am today by the grace of God. He transformed my life into a new beginning with blessings, favor, grace, and his goodness. God gave me a new life to help other women who are being abused, living in bondage, struggling with who they are, living in a defeated mentality, or who have never accepted Jesus as their Lord and Savior. My testimony is only an instrument to bless so many women and to bring glory to our Heavenly Father. I am our Heavenly Father's vessel to be used as a blessing to others. Every day is a new day to be a blessing to someone. I claim and confess that every person who reads this book will be touched by God's healing power and that every heart will receive all that God has in store for them. In Matthew 13:15-16, "For this people's heart is waxed gross, and their ears are dull of hearing, and their eyes they have closed; lest at any time they should see with their eyes, and hear with their ears, and should understand with their heart, and should be converted, and I should heal them. But blessed are your eyes, for they see: and your ears, for they hear." Open your ears to hear, your eyes to see, and your heart to understand the transformation that God has done in my life and the transformation he can make happen in your life.

Up until I was the age of 16, Kyle witnessed and listened to me being physically, mentally, and verbally abused. The environment I lived in was negative and full of darkness. My life was filled with frustration, anger, sadness, depression, and fear. I would walk around with a smile to attempt to hide and deny the pain and the anger that was within. My fake smile hid the tears of loneliness and fear. My life was filled with darkness and anger. I was lost and dead. I didn't trust anyone and I walked around worrying about what people thought of me. The Devil used people to speak negative, hurtful, and ugly words to condemn and judge me. Satan attacked my mind by reciting and playing the hurtful and harsh words through my family and people I crossed paths with. I found myself listening, believing, and acting out those lies from the pit of hell. There were plenty of nights that I would lie down on the floor of bedroom trembling with tears of rejection and hurt. I attempted to share with my family but they thought I was crazy and acting out for attention. They could not understand me because they were living their lives with the same troubles, hurt, and pain from their past. My family was broken in their hearts from the hurts, pain, and wounds from their childhood. Now I know, they needed Jesus to come into heart and receive their healing through the blood of the lamb. I watched them fall and stay down, but I made a decision to get back up. When

I pressed forward, I may have fallen once or twice or even multiple times, but I stood with courage and refused to give up. I am glad and blessed that God put determination and courage in me to overcome the obstacles that I would have to face. In the midst of the storms, God sent his angels to guard and preserve my path. In Psalms 91:10-11, "There shall no evil befall thee, neither shall any plague come nigh thy dwelling. For he shall give his angels charge over thee, to keep thee in all of thy ways." I know God had his angels protect and shield me from dangerous and brutal situations.

During my childhood, I remember the times when my mother's boyfriend would beat us until we could not stand. One day I was in my bedroom (the room that I thought I could escape from the abuse); my mom's boyfriend came into my room with an angry and haughty look on his face. If you ever walked in my bedroom, you would find my curtains nailed to the windows, locks broken off the doors, and a peep hole for someone to look within. I never quite understood why he did the things he did. Also, I remember whenever he caught us looking out of a window he would come storming in our room and start yelling at us. I could see the fear, anger, and darkness in his eyes. His eyes were filled with hatred, ugliness, and pride. I believe it is a gift that I can look in people's eyes and see their heart! His heart was filled with unforgiveness, pain, hurt, anger, bitterness, resentment, fear, worry, and hatred. God showed me how important it is to have a pure and loving heart! In Matthew 12:34-35, "O generation of vipers, how can you, being evil, speak good things? for out of the abundance of the heart the mouth speaketh. A good man out of the good treasure of the heart bringeth forth good things: and an evil man out of the evil treasure bringeth forth evil things." I learned how not to live your life with a sin-conscious and an unclean heart. Moreover, it is so important to humble yourself before the Lord, turn from your wicked ways, and pray for God to give you humility. I depend, rely, lean, and trust in the Lord for everything! In Proverbs 3:5-6, "Trust in the Lord with all of your heart; and lean not unto your own understanding. In all of your ways acknowledge him, and he shall direct your paths." The Lord has been and is so faithful in my life!

To be honest, I don't know my mom's boyfriend's story, but I do know that through Jesus Christ you can be saved and healed. God can change anyone, but they have to be willing to accept change and correction. In Proverbs 12:1, "Whoso loveth instruction loveth knowledge: but he that hateth reproof is brutish." My mom's boyfriend despised correction and it even provoked him to get angrier. There was an incident where he went into my brother's room and started picking on him. I couldn't take it anymore so I stood up and went into my brother's room. I told him to stop and to leave my brother alone. Since I was a child, God has given me boldness and courage. I never backed down when I knew something was wrong. In 1 Timothy 6:12, "Fight the good fight of faith, lay hold on eternal life, whereunto thou art also called, and hast professed a good profession before many witnesses." I have always fought the good fight of faith, especially for my loved ones. I am known to protect, nurture, care, love, and defend for the ones close to me.

Furthermore, my mom's boyfriend started grabbing and spitting in my face. All of a sudden, my brother came forward with a pair of scissors. I thought my brother was going to stab him. My mom's boyfriend loosed his grip on my arm and provoked my brother to stab him, but he refused to. I could see the anger in my brother's eyes and the fear in my mom's boyfriend's eyes. It really shook my mom's boyfriend and he was astounded at my brother's action. So many ugly things happened from the time I was a baby to the age 19, but I only focus on the good things that God has done in my life. It is very difficult to share with you everything that has happened in my life. There are some things that I refuse to remember.

Anyways, I have been known to never give up on anything and to never stop fighting for what you know is right. God gave me boldness to take a stand and encourage my mom's boyfriend to stop hurting us. There was times when he felt intimidated and disgusted by my actions. My mom would allow him to criticize, hurt, and bring her down to his level, which was a defeated mentality. I refused to be treated badly and I believe in treating people the way you want to be treated. In Matthew 7:12, "Therefore all things whatsoever you would that men should do to you, do you even so to them: for this is the law and the prophets." The Golden Rule is to do unto others the way you want them to do for you. I faced brutal consequences for taking a stand. When my mom's boyfriend pushed my mom and my brother down the stairs, I spoke to him with conviction and confidence. It lit a fuse off in him to see me so strong. He desired to weaken the people in his life. As I recall, he ran down the stairs and stepped on my mom and brother to grab me, but I was already running out the door. I could hear him yelling and threatening to hurt me if I didn't come back, but I knew better. My heart was beating through my chest, my mind was racing with so many thoughts, and my body was aching from the exhaustion of running full force. I ran into our neighbor's house and immediately recognized that nobody was home. I ran out of the house and headed to the woods. I knew that I had to find a place to hide and it had to be quick. I could hear the anger and ugliness in mom's boyfriend's voice. It was evil and wicked. I knew he was getting close so I jumped into a bush and sat there with stillness. Immediately I placed my head on my knees and asked God to help me. I was so terrified and sacred. I heard my mom's boyfriend walk by, and then drive off in his truck to attempt to find me. When he drove off, my body started to tremble with emotions and fear. I was scared for my family and I didn't know what his next move was going to be. I sat there until my mother came looking for me.

There were some incidents when I would stay in the same spot for over eight hours. If I knew a situation was getting out of control, I would get up and start running for an escape, but there were times when my mom's boyfriend prevented me from entering the escape route. It was horrific and exhausting when he would catch any of my family members. Every day he would find something to fight or complain about. For 18 years, my brother and I had to face obstacles and overcome things that nobody should have to go through, but I thank God that he has turned our ashes to beauty. In Isaiah 61:3, "To appoint unto them that mourn in Zion, to give unto them beauty for ashes, the oil of joy for mourning, the garment of praise for the spirit of heaviness; that they might be called trees of righteousness, the planting of the Lord, that he might be glorified." God answered my prayers and rescued us. That was the first time I saw God show up in a HUGE and GREATER way!

My mom dropped my brother and I off at our grandparent's house and told us she couldn't take it anymore. My mom insisted that she needed to go back and help him with his anger management. I never thought the woman who carried us for 9 months would choose her abusive boyfriend over us. The feeling of abandonment felt like a knife punctuated my heart. The stinging and pain of a stab causes layers of wounds. Later on, I recognized and realized that God rescued my brother and I from the unstable, abusive situation. God used my grandparents and aunt and uncle to take us in. I give God all of the glory for being the woman I am today!

Today, I know that God loves me and Jesus loves me. God loves you and he loves you as much as he loves Jesus. His love is unconditional and he is a forgiving God. In 1 Corinthians 13:8, "Love never fails..." God is love and God never fails. He pours his love upon us and he loves us so much that he gave us Jesus. In John 3:16, "For God so loved the world that he gave us his begotten son, whosoever believes in his Son shall not perish, but have everlasting life." God loves me so much that he continues to pour his blessings into my life.

In June 2007, I became a new creature in Christ. I remembered that day as if were yesterday. My life was falling apart and I was clinging on everything I could get my hands on. I was holding on to my past and living in a negative mindset. I walked around with fear and anger. I had the mindset that something bad was going to happen. I would look in the mirror and thoughts of ugliness, destruction, unworthiness, and frustration would attack my mind. I began living out those thoughts and when somebody would say, "You are beautiful and loved." I would cast it down and walk with defeat. All of that changed with I accepted Jesus as my Lord and Savior.

On that day, I was working in the guidance department of my high school and I was feeling depressed and discouraged. At the time, a high school student, Andrew Harrison who worked in the guidance department pulled out a Bible from his backpack. He came over and handed me the Bible. He said, "Do you promise to read the Bible every day?" I said, "Yes." I didn't realize what I had agreed to. I recognized that I had experienced a suddenly. I had never received a Bible until that day. I had always wanted my own Bible to study and God knew the desires of my heart. When I got home, I closed my bedroom door and I burst out in tears because only God knew I wanted my own Bible. I recognized and captured that it was a gift from God. He truly cared about me and he loved me. God was always there and he heard every prayer. My whole life I felt like nobody was listening to me and I felt alone, but that day God revealed to me that I was never alone. In Joshua 1:5, "There shall not any man be able to stand before thee all the days of thy life: as I was with Moses, so I will be with thee: I will not fail thee, not forsake thee." God will never leave you nor forsake you.

At that very moment, God had softened my heart and captured my attention. When, I entered my bedroom, I knelt down and opened my heart to receive Jesus Christ. I said aloud, "Dear Heavenly Father, forgive me for all of my sins and cleanse me from all unrighteousness. Jesus come into my heart and take my life and do something with it. I receive you, Jesus as my Lord and Savior. In Jesus Name, Amen." When I accepted Jesus as my Lord and Savior, a HUGE load was lifted off of me and I could feel his presence. The darkness was filled with light. I felt peace and comfort. I could feel his lovely arms wrapped around me. I am set free and no longer held captive under the Devil's authority. In Romans 8:15, "For ye have not received the spirit of bondage again to fear; but ye have received the Spirit of adoption, whereby we cry, Abba, Father." My true freedom is in Christ Jesus. I am God's beloved child and the righteousness of God. God loves me no matter what and his love is unconditional. I became a new creature in Christ Jesus. In 2 Corinthians 5:17, "Therefore if any man be in Christ, he is a new creature: old things have passed away; behold, all things are become new." Every day I thank God for his grace and mercy. He is a forgiving God and he loves each one of us. He loves us as much as he loves Jesus. God is my Daddy and my Father. I know no matter what I go through, he is already there!

I am born again in Christ and I am a child of God. The enemy tries to use people and things to bring me back to that day were I felt defeated and condemned, but I know that I have authority over the Devil. In John 10:10, "The thief come not, but to steal, kill, and destroy: but I came that they might have life, and that they might have it more abundantly." There are times when the enemy will try to control my mind with thoughts from my past or bring up my past through the words of others, but I know that I am a new creature in Christ Jesus and the greater one is living inside me.

Every day I renew my mind according to the word of God. In Romans 12:2, "And be not conformed to this world: but be ye transformed by the renewing of your mind, that ye may prove what is that good, and acceptable, and perfect, will of God." The enemy tries to tempt or distract me, but the Holy Spirit will remind me to walk in love. In Genesis 1:28, "And God blessed them, and God said unto them, be fruitful, multiply, replenish the earth, and subdue it: and have dominion over the fish of the sea, and over the fowl of the air, and over every living thing that move upon the earth." I know that I have dominion over every living thing. Through Jesus Christ, I have authority over the enemy and I denounce the past and everything the Devil stands on. In Galatians 5:22, "The fruit of the Spirit is love, peace, faith, hope, gentleness, meekness, temperance, goodness, longsuffering, joy, and self-control." I strive to be like Jesus, act like Jesus, talk like Jesus, and think like Jesus.

I thank God for the life he has given me. I am thankful for the many blessings in my life. He has given me his love, he has forgiven me, and he loves me no matter what. I am grateful for the family that God has given me and my wonderful, blessed husband, Kyle Moore who continued to operate in God's love (agape). I thank God for giving me the courage and strength to forgive those who have hurt and mistreated me. I would not be standing here today if it wasn't for God's grace. I am blessed and confident in the

Lord. In Mark 11:22, "And Jesus answering saith unto them, have faith in God." I put my faith and trust in God that he will continue to use me to be a blessing to others.

Every day, I look to our Heavenly Father for direction, guidance, wisdom, and knowledge to help those that need to know Jesus. Since I have accepted Jesus as my Lord and Savior, my life has been restored, renewed, and healed. I give God all the glory for the good things in my life. He is faithful and true to his word. If you haven't accepted Jesus as your Lord and Savior, please come forward and get to know Jesus. He loves you and he cares for you. Jesus knows your pain and the anger that you keep hidden inside of you. He is ready for you to cast your cares unto him and for you to let him come into your heart. Jesus is your Deliverer, Healer, Comforter, Security, Refugee, and Buckler. Say after me, "Jesus I ask you to forgive me of all of my sins and cleanse me from all unrighteousness. I open my heart to you Jesus and I accept you, Jesus as my Lord and Savior. Use me to be a blessing to others and take my life and do something with it. I thank for you, Father for loving and caring for me. I cast all of my cares unto you and I am a new creature in Christ. I thank you, Father for all of the good things in my life. I am blessed, healed, and made whole in you. I follow you Jesus to the promise land. I praise and honor you, Jesus. In the Mighty Name of Jesus, Amen." You are now a born-again believer in Christ Jesus! Find and attend a faith-filled church near you! Read your bible daily and meditate in the word of God day and night!

Continue to read on and enjoy the writings of my new life in Christ Jesus… Writings straight from the heart of a woman who never gave up… A heart of a woman who believes in Jesus…Open the door to your heart… Capture… Embrace… Expect and believe God will transform you inside and out through these writings…From the heart of Jesus…I included these writings to encourage and remind you - You Are More Than An Over comer…Don't let your circumstances or people tell you otherwise…

God has a Purpose for Your Life

✝

"The Lord will fulfill (his purpose) for me; your love, O LORD, endures forever-do not abandon the works of your hands."

Psalm 138:8

We may not understand why God has us do certain things. For example, the Holy Spirit leads you to speak, "Jesus loves you," in a woman's ear or to stop in the middle of the road and lead a homeless person to Jesus Christ. He has a purpose for everything. In order to follow Jesus, we have to be obedient and hearken to the voice of the Lord. We can miss our great opportunities if we fail to listen to the Holy Spirit. Open your eyes to recognize those moments; the moments he gives you can be your greatest blessings. Instead of questioning God, say, "Father, your will be done. I fully trust you and I stand on your word. I will follow your instructions." In Matthew 6:9-13, "After this manner therefore pray ye: Our Father which art in heaven, Hallowed be thy name. Thy kingdom come. Thy will be done in earth, as it is heaven. Give us this day our daily bread. And forgive us our debts, as we forgive our debtors. And lead us not into temptation, but deliver us from evil: For thine is the kingdom, and the power, and the glory, for ever. Amen." Walk in the Spirit and you will see things happen in the supernatural realm. The Holy Spirit is our Comforter, Advocate, Security, Protector, Teacher, and Instructor. In John 16:13, "Howbeit when he, the Spirit of truth, is come, he will guide you into all truth: for he shall not speak of himself; but whatsoever he shall hear, that shall he speak: and he will show you things to come." He guides us, teaches us, and brings all things to our remembrance.

Do you know the Holy Spirit will lead you to the right place at the right time? God has a master plan for our lives and there are people in our lives who need Jesus. Our obedience to be led by the Holy Spirit exemplifies our love for God. Through our actions, we reveal the image of Jesus and people can see him in us. We are who we are in Christ Jesus. We are lost and dead without God. There are people in our lives who have Jesus in their heart, but have fallen to the waste side. They are blinded and deceived by the enemy. One foot is in the kingdom and the other foot is in the world's system. It is our responsibility as the body of Christ to take a stand and command the Devil to get underneath our feet. In James 4:7, "Submit yourselves to God; resist the Devil and he shall flee from you." We are God's people and we have authority as God's children.

Throughout your life, can you identify the times when God used you to reveal his goodness? I can remember several occasions when God poured out his goodness and mercy onto his people. For example, he instructed me to reach out and pray for a woman who was distraught, confused, broken, held captive, and full of fear. It is our responsibility to listen and be obedient. When we put him first, then he can operate in our lives and those around us. In Matthew 6:33, "Seek first the kingdom of God and his righteousness; all these other things shall be added unto you." By putting God first place, he was able to use me as his instrument. God gave me specific instructions to listen to the woman of brokenness and to pray with her for the manifestation of God to be released into her life. We agreed for resurrection in her marriage, finances, relationships, and job. We claimed for supernatural financial provision and for her healing from the crown of her head to the soles of her feet. In Matthew 18:19, "Again I say unto you, that if two of you shall agree on earth as touching anything that they shall ask, it shall be done for them of my father which is in heaven." There is power in the agreement of prayer. I believe it has already been done in the Name of Jesus. It is finished and completed. I know this encounter is part of God's plan. He is bringing his people together to enhance and build his kingdom. It is very important for each of us to be obedient because we have a responsibility in the kingdom of God.

God is bigger than anything we can ever imagine. In Ephesians 3:19-20, "And to know the love of Christ, which passeth knowledge, that ye might be filled with all the fullness of God. Now unto him that is able to do exceeding abundantly above all that we ask or think, according to the power that worketh in us." His ways and thoughts are higher than ours. There is no other God like Jehovah. He loves us so much that he gives us things to enjoy. He is no respector of persons. Recognize and capture his purpose for your life. He has called and chosen us because he loves us. Surrender yourself to Jesus, so he can use you to be a blessing to others. Make a decision to consistently stand on God's word. In consistency, lies the power and leads to progressive increase. His word is a lamp to our feet. In Psalm 119: 105, "Thy word is a lamp unto my feet, and a light unto my path." When we are rooted and grounded in his word, then he can shine through us. In Ephesians 3:17, "That Christ may dwell in your hearts by faith; that ye, being rooted and grounded in love." Let God's light shine through you. In Matthew 5:13-14, "Ye are the salt of the earth: but if the salt has lost his savour, wherewith shall it be salted? It is thenceforth good for nothing, but to be cast out, and to be trodden under foot of men. Ye are the light of the world. A city that is set on a hill cannot be hid." We are the righteousness of God and we are to come boldly before the throne of grace. Fear not, believe only, and you will be made whole. Stand up for God's kingdom and follow Jesus to the promise land. There is great reward in the promise land. Keep your eyes on Jesus for he is the prize. In Philippians 3:13-14, "Brethren, I count not myself to have apprehended: but this one thing I do, forgetting those things which are behind, and reaching forth unto those things which are before. I press toward the mark for the prize of the high calling of God in Christ Jesus." Don't look back! Instead, look forward and keep your eyes lifted up! Worry looks around, but faith looks up and rises above the circumstances. Give yourself to Jesus and let him come in to your heart. God's kingdom is where you want your feet planted. Remain fixed on the word of God and be not moved by your circumstances. Rest in Jesus for he is the Prince of Peace. In Isaiah 9:6, "For unto us a child is born, unto us a son is given: and the government shall be upon his shoulder: and his name shall be called Wonderful, Counselor, The mighty God, The everlasting

Father, and The Prince of Peace." Keep the word before your eyes and in your ears at all times. Your time is here and the victory is yours! Go forward in living a victorious life with purpose and direction from our Heavenly Father! Be obedient and follow Jesus with your whole heart!

Now, you know God has a purpose for your life. Make a decision today to trust and believe him. Don't turn back to the way things use to be…Start a new beginning…Fresh start with a spirit of excellence…Continue to read on and be inspired by how Kyle and I trusted God by taking steps of obedience toward his plan for our lives…

God Is the Most Highest

†

"I will be glad and rejoice in thee: I will sing praise to thy name, O thou most High."
Psalm 9:2

I remember the day when my husband and I decided to follow God's master plan. It seems like it was yesterday. Our whole lives changed when we stood in agreement to trust God and never look back. We confessed that we would never go back to the way it was before. My husband, Kyle Moore and I stood on Philippians 4:19 and Matthew 6:33. We believed and knew God had something special in store for us. We could sense it in our spirit. Kyle and I are overwhelmed with tears of joy when we talk or think about it. By the grace of God, we are who we are and where we are today. My desire is to take this time and share with you the moment that changed the rest of our lives.

On April 4, 2011, I woke up from a dream and it was a dream like never before. I still remember the dream. In the dream, I was working with New York Life and I was asking my husband if he knew anybody who would value my work. He replied, "Ask mom if she knows anybody. I am sure she will be able to help you." In the dream, I was seeking for clients and I saw myself wearing business attire. As I recall, I was still working at the bank when I had this dream. I knew there was a reason for the dream and I knew that it would come to pass. I knew God had revealed it to me for a purpose. I could sense it coming alive in my spirit. God had instructed me to share the dream with Kyle only because he would stand in agreement and he was part of God's plan. It is very important to go to God first because he will reveal to you the people that will stand in agreement. Only God knows who we need in our lives and he brings the right people in our lives to see us succeed and prosper.

After I had the dream, I was at a stop sign in my parking lot when I heard the voice of the Lord. His voice caught my attention and he spoke with love and compassion. The Lord said these words, "It is time." I asked him, "Lord, what do you mean?" He said, "It is time for your next assignment." God revealed to me that I had accomplished the assignment at the bank. Also, he wanted to see if I trusted him and relied on him to help me.

Later that evening, I asked God, "How do I share this with my husband?" I asked God for wisdom and knowledge. I sat down right next to Kyle on the bed and I shared with him that God said it was time to leave the bank. At the time when the Lord spoke to me, I was going to school full-time and working at the bank part-time. Kyle was laid off from his job. I fully trusted God and believed in his word. I knew that he had something far better in store for us. God wanted to lift us up to a higher level. He had a plan with many blessings. Jesus wanted Kyle and I to follow him towards the promise land filled with milk and honey. Jesus loves us so much and God loves us as much as he loves Jesus.

When I shared with Kyle what the Lord had spoken to me, I found out that the Lord had spoke to him too. Kyle said, "Do what the Lord says? I am in agreement with you." I said to Kyle, "The Lord spoke to you too." He smiled and hugged me. Tears of joy and new beginning poured out of me. I knew the things that are seen are temporary, but the things that are not seen are eternal. In Psalms 23:1, "The Lord is my Shepherd (to feed, guide, and shield me), I shall not lack." Kyle and I walked by faith and not by sight! We stepped out with faith in God! Kyle and I stood on the word of God! We were fully persuaded what God had promised, he is faithful to perform it. Kyle and I put our trust in the Lord. We knew God is our source and our provider. In Philippians 4:19, "But my God shall supply all your need according to his riches in glory by Christ Jesus." He is our Jehovah Jireh. He is our security and our protector.

In October 2011, we experienced God's supernatural favor and explosive blessings. The act of obedience opened doors of HUGE opportunities. In Romans 5:19, "For as by one man's disobedience many were made sinners, so by the obedience of one shall many be made righteous." God opens doors that no man can shut. Kyle received a call from W.O. Grubb to come in and submit an application!!! Few days later, Kyle started his career path with W.O. Grubb.

The reason I am sharing this with you, Kyle and I prayed, sowed seeds, and thanked God for the position at W.O. Grubb for six years before it came to pass! I remember Kyle sharing with me that he saw himself operating a crane with a hard hat and wearing a W.O. Grubb logo! Kyle held on to the vision that the Lord revealed to him through his spiritual eyes. I watched Kyle every day grow stronger and stronger in his faith in God! God was teaching me a lesson through Kyle! He taught both of us to stand on the word of God and to not let your faith waver. In James 1:6, "But let him ask in faith, nothing wavering. For he that wavereth is like a wave of the sea driven with the wind and tossed." Kyle and I placed our faith and trust in God. I truly believe God allowed everything to happen earlier on in our marriage so that Kyle and I would enjoy the land of plenty and abundance.

Every day we look to God first for and about everything. The enemy tries to tempt us with living independently from God, condemnation, and defeated mentality, but we know the word of God is our weapon. Kyle and I speak God's word to the enemy! We command the enemy to get underneath our feet in the Name of Jesus. In James 4:7, "We submit ourselves to God, therefore; resist the Devil and he shall flee from you." In John 10:10, "The thief comes only in order to steal and kill and destroy. Jesus came that we may have and enjoy life, and have it in abundance (to the full, till it overflows)." Kyle and I believe and stand on God's word. In John 14:6, "Jesus saith unto him, I am the way, the truth, and the life: no man cometh unto the Father, but by me." God has always been faithful and true to his word. We committed ourselves to follow Jesus for the rest of our lives. God has poured his blessings upon us. We took, received, claimed, and owned what God has promised us. In Psalms 23:6, "Surely goodness, mercy, and unfailing love shall follow me all the days of my life, and through the length of my days the house of the Lord (and his presence) shall be my dwelling place." God is for and with me all the time.

In Romans 8:31, "What shall we then say to these things? If God be for us, who can be against us?" It doesn't matter what other people think! It only matters what God says!

I leave this with you; God will never leave you nor forsake you. He cares for you and he knows everything about you. He understands what you are going through, but he doesn't want you to go through it alone. When you fall, he will lift you up. When you are weak, he will carry you and strengthen you. When you cry, he will wipe your tears. When you feel alone, know he is already there comforting you. When you are troubled, he will protect you. When you are scared, he will secure you from all harm. When you are depressed, he will give you joy. When you feel unloved, know Jesus loves you and God loves you. When you feel like giving up, know your breakthrough is here. When you are down in the pit, know your victory is here and you are more than a conqueror. Stand strong in the Lord and declare and take your victory. You are a child of God. Come to your Heavenly Father with child-like faith and he will restore you. He is your refugee and buckler. Declare you are the righteous hand of God. You are a victor and not a victim. Believe your day is here and confess Jesus is your Lord and Savior. The Prince of Peace is within in you. Jesus is alive!!!

By following Jesus Christ and making him the center of your life, there is purpose and goodness to enjoy…Open your heart and receive God's goodness…Kyle and I are witnesses to how good God truly is…Continue to read on and learn about the good things we experienced by staying focused on our Heavenly Father…

God's Goodness Is Upon You

✝

"Oh that men would praise the Lord for his goodness, and for his wonderful works to the children of men!"
Psalm 107:21

We are so blessed and it is all because of God. Expect God's goodness in your life. Give thanksgiving for all of the blessings in your life. Identify him as an Awesome and Mighty God! He is victorious and strong. Give God all the glory for all of the good things in your life. You are here today because of him. Think back at the times where God rescued you or turned a situation around in your favor. In Romans 8:28, "And we know that all things work together for good to them that love God, to them who are called according to his purpose." God rewards us with good things. In Proverbs 3:4, "So shalt thou find favor and good understanding in the sight of God and man." He is faithful and true to his word. God is a Big God. When you are facing a storm or circumstance that looks impossible, know and believe that with God all things are possible. In Luke 1:37, "For with God nothing shall be impossible." He turns the impossible into possible.

Can you remember a time in your life where God gave you a break or helped you in an impossible situation? When I was 16 years old, God took me out of a difficult situation that seemed impossible in the natural, but in the supernatural God was putting the right people in my path and preparing me for my exit. God gave me strength, courage, confidence, and grace to rise and take a stand. I thank God today that I am free from bondage and abuse, delivered from the power of the enemy, healed from the crown of my head to the soles of my feet, confident to be who I am in Christ, secure in his presence, courageous to take a stand for Christ Jesus, and beautiful in the image of who he is. God can take you places where you never dreamed of and take you to a higher level. Do you trust God for good breaks and blessings to pour into your lie? Are you giving God something BIG to work with? You serve a BIG God! In Colossians 3:23-24, "And whatsoever you do, do it heartily, as to the Lord, and not unto men; knowing that of the Lord you shall receive the reward of the inheritance: for you serve the Lord Christ." He is waiting for you to take the next BIG step. Receive and recognize God's goodness in your life. Give him the glory and get ready for God to work through you. He is already there!

Every day, wake up with the expectancy of God's goodness upon your life. Speak and confess God's goodness in your life. Get ready for God to bring something BIG in your life. Develop a mindset that something good is about to happen. Dwell and meditate on God's word day and night. In Psalms 91:1, "He that dwells in the secret place shall abide under the shadow of the Almighty." God protects us from harm and rewards us for our diligence. In Hebrews 11:6, "But without faith it is impossible to please him: for he that cometh to God must believe that he is, and that he is a rewarder of them that diligently seek him." He longs for us to spend time with him so he can refresh and rejuvenate us for the next BIG step that is out in front of us. God is a good God. He only gives us the best of the best. God loves you so much. Know and understand who he is.

Do you recall the great opportunities that God released in your life? Are you aware and alert of God's goodness in my life? When you receive a good news report, do you automatically without even thinking about it, give God the glory? Who is receiving the credit and recognition for the good things in your life? You? Your spouse? Your supervisor? Your teacher? Your mentor? Stay focused on God and claim good things over you and your household. In Joshua 24:15, "As for me and my household, we will serve the Lord all of the days of our lives." Put God first place in your life and watch him continue to bring blessings into your life.

According to Psalms 23:6, "Surely goodness and mercy shall follow me all the days of my life: and I will dwell in the house of the Lord forever." Move forward with God and trust him no matter what. Rest and abide in your Lord Jesus Christ. He will give you peace and comfort in your most challenging times. In Mark 4:39-40, "Peace, be still. And the wind ceased, and there was a great calm. And he said unto them, why are you so fearful? How is it that you have no faith?" Walk by faith and not by sight. In 2 Corinthians 5:7, "For we walk by faith, not by sight." Keep your eyes and ears open for God's goodness. Don't miss the opportunity to admire and embrace God's blessings.

When you are going through a storm, do you fall into a depression and disappointment or do you believe for God's best? Worship and praise your Heavenly

Father. In 1 Peter 5:5, "Casting all your care upon him; for he careth for you." Your Daddy cares for you and wants the absolute best for his beloved children. God gives us the ability, talent, and gift to move forward with him. He knows everything about us and he is here to bless and prosper us. God is for you, who can be against you? Take a stand today and confess that you will only receive God's best! Live boldly and enhance the kingdom of God! Watch and experience God going to work in your life. Submit to God's will and not your will. In Matthew 6:10, "Thy kingdom come. Thy will be done in earth, as it is in heaven." You are a blessed child of God! Live and soak in God's unlimited goodness. Marinate and absorb the lasting taste of God's abundance in your life.

Now, you know that God has a purpose, plan, and good things in store for you and your family but sometimes we take life for granted…Every is going good until you come across a bump in the road…Kyle and I have experienced many bumps and u-turns in our journey with the Lord… Continue to read on and learn how Kyle and I overcome life challenges by holding on to Jesus…

Life Is a Gift from Our Heavenly Father

†

"The thief cometh not, but for to steal, and to kill, and to destroy: I am come that they might have life, and they might have it more abundantly."
John 10:10

On May 19, 2011, was not just any day but the day that unlocked the door of newness and victory. A beautiful sunny day filled with God's blessings, goodness, and favor! The day I graduated from Virginia Commonwealth University with a Bachelors of Science in Finance. That moment is now stored in my keepsake box that reminds me of how BIG our God really is. The reason I am sharing this day with you is not because I graduated from Virginia Commonwealth University but the challenges and obstacles that I had to overcome to be where I am today.

During the four years of my education, I went to school full-time, worked part-time, involved in networking organizations, married my day care sweetheart, Kyle Moore, and watched God perform a Miracle through my Dad. In January 2008, my Dad at the age of 40 had a massive aneurism that changed not only his life but the people who came in contact with our family. That day I found out how precious life truly is. I never thought that something like that would be so life-changing. I realized that I had to get rid of the two words "I thought" out of my vocabulary. I started to seek God and ask him what is it that you want me to learn. Also, I asked God to give me the strength and confidence to focus on his purpose for my life.

God told me that I needed to keep focusing on him and trust him to carry me through this situation. When I trusted him, I started to enjoy life and I found peace in the midst of the storm. In Jeremiah 17:7, "Blessed is the man that trusteth in the Lord, and whose hope the Lord is." Through the storm, I knew that I had to move forward and be a blessing to others. God revealed to me that I needed to be strong for my family and to speak encouraging words into their lives. Through those times, I was faced with challenges, struggles, pain, and frustration, and then the Lord spoke to me about how I needed to cast my cares unto him.

As I recall, people were asking me, "How did you stay so strong while your Dad had a stroke?" and "How were you able to handle married life, work, and school while your Dad was in the hospital?" My answer was "By the grace of God." By his grace, I was able to overcome obstacles and face challenges, and still remain as a victor. In John 16:33, "These things I have spoken unto ye that in me you might have peace. In the world ye shall have tribulation: but be of good cheer; I have overcome the world." Every person that I meet I speak positive words into their life because I was at the point in my life where I knew nothing, but anger, pain, and hurt. My desire is for God's people to know that while we are here for appointed time, we need to be thankful for the things that God has given us to richly enjoy. In 1 Timothy 6:17, "Charge them that are rich in this world, that they be not high minded, not trust in uncertain riches, but in the living God, who giveth us richly all things to enjoy."

Wake up every day thanking our Heavenly Father for your loved ones and for bringing you through the trouble times. Also, thank him for the things that he has in store for you and know that what he has in store for you and your household is the best. God only gives you the best!

I am blessed and thankful that God had opened my eyes through my Dad's stroke recovery process. God taught me that life is a gift from him to enjoy and to not take this precious life that he has given us for granted. By watching my Dad take his first steps all over again, I started to appreciate and thank God for EVERYTHING. Every day I speak blessings over my family and friends. I thank God for giving me a second chance to enjoy my time with my Dad. I thank God for calling me to help and encourage women and children with confidence, determination, and motivation. I thank God for the blessings that he has given my husband and I. I thank him for restoration in relationships, renewal of marriages, divine health, abundance, prosperity, wisdom, knowledge, ability to learn, to go though challenges, strength to keep pressing forward, courage to take a stand, to believe all things are possible, and to see dreams come true.

I look at graduating from Virginia Commonwealth University as a new chapter in my life and an opportunity to receive things that I would not have even imagined. In Ephesians 3:20, "Now unto him that is able to do exceeding abundantly above all that we ask or think, according to the power that worketh in us." I believe this is a stepping stone to what is ahead and God will direct my every step towards his purpose for my life. I know this is the beginning of God's goodness and blessings. The challenges that I face will only make me stronger in the Lord and prepare me for an abundant life.

Overall, I encourage each one of you to live life with thanksgiving, love, happiness, and laughter. Be a blessing to others and find someone to give a compliment to. Believe God that all things are possible. In Mark 9:23, "Jesus said unto him, if thou canst believe, all things are possible to him that believeth." Trust and have faith in God that he working on your behalf to turn the situation around. Love others the way God loves you. In Mark 11:26, "And when ye stand praying, forgive, if ye have ought against any: that your Father also which is in heaven may forgive you your trespasses. But if ye do not forgive, neither will your Father which is in heaven forgive your trespasses." Forgive yourself and others. Live life to the fullest and enjoy it. You are who you are and where you are today because of the choices and decisions you made. God is in control. Jesus loves you, so stop trying to earn his love. Be thankful for your family and learn to cherish every moment with them. Remember always: never take your life for granted and believe that all things are possible!!!

Today is your day to invest and believe in who you are in Christ…Kyle and I have learned the value and worth we are in Christ Jesus…The world will tell you otherwise but through God's eyes we are made perfect in Christ…Read how Kyle and I captured the significance of believing…

Invest In Yourself, Believe In Who You Are
†

"Jesus said unto him, If you can believe, all things are possible to him that believe."
Mark 9:23

When you get up in the morning, what do you see in the mirror? Do you know who you are? What is your purpose in life? Do you value or believe in who you are? Are you investing in yourself? We all have been given a greater purpose, but what are we doing with it? Sometimes we wait and look around for things to change, but really it is within ourselves that need to change. Often times, we reflect on our childhood, our past relationships, or our environment as an excuse for why we responded or acted the way we did towards a situation. In 2 Corinthians 4:18, "While we look not at the things which are seen, but at the things which are not seen: for the things which are seen are temporal; but the things which are not seen are eternal." We have to look above and beyond our circumstance and know that it is only temporary. Sometimes, we are put to the test to see if you are really ready to take the next step towards victory. In order to live a victorious life, you have to believe and know who you are in Christ Jesus.

Life is about being a blessing to others. Do you wake up in the morning and seek for someone to be a blessing to? If not, then start today. One word or smile or phone call can change someone's life. When my Dad had a stroke in January 2008, I realized how important it is to build relationships and to stay connected with each other. My Dad taught me how to walk in love, set goals that are achievable, believe all things are possible, never give up on anything, cherish your time with your family, put your best in all that you do, and keep those special loved ones in your life to watch you grow.

Through my Dad's stroke recovery process, I learned there will be times when you fall, but you have to get right back up. I watched my Dad fall and struggle to stand, but he never stopped trying and he refused to give up. I watched him go full force with confidence, determination, motivation, and courage. It made me realize that in life you will face trials and tribulations, but know in your heart that everything is going to be alright! Go about life with a winning attitude and a stature as an over comer of all obstacles.

My Dad reminded me that you can do anything that you set your mind to and to face every challenge with an "I CAN" attitude. In Philippians 4:13, "I can do all things through Christ Jesus who strengthens me." If you are passionate about making a difference in your community, then get out of your comfortable zone and take action. Do some research and connect with someone who can help you pursue your passion. If you are seeking for wisdom and knowledge, go to the word of God and seek direction towards a higher education or new opportunities to expand on career training. My Dad always encouraged and pushed me to get a higher education and I am blessed to say that I had a parent who believed in who I am. You may think why am I doing this or why am I spending all of this money for education? Believe me when I say that you are investing in yourself and your family's future. You are growing, maturing, and developing right before your eyes. You may not understand now or you may not see the change, but remember how far you have come. You are in a greater position than you were year ago. In Romans 8:37, "Nay, in all these things we are more than conquerors through him that loved us." You are more than a conqueror. You are a victor not a victim. Never go back to the way things once were; keep moving forward you are so close to receiving your rewards. You will face opposition, but keep your eyes on the reward that is right in front of you. In Proverbs 4:23, "Keep thy heart with all diligence; for out of it are the issues of life." Guard your heart and stand strong. Take it, receive it, have it, claim it, and own your rewards. Resist discouragement, fear, and lack of confidence. If you face rejection, then know that there is something far better in store for you. Surround yourself with positive people who desire to see you succeed and prosper. Look around and identify those that are speaking life into you such as a professor, mentor, leader, or family member. Are you listening to people with a negative outlook in life? Poor-me attitude? Wishful-thinking attitude? Ask God to remove those people from your circle and replace them with God-fearing believers who will uplift and encourage you to be who you are in Christ Jesus. Refuse to let people talk you out of your God-given dreams. The enemy may attempt to speak through the ones close to you but don't believe the lies. The enemy is the father of lies. You only believe the word of God. Don't believe anything contrary to the word of God. Be alert and cautious of your surroundings and what you are listening to. Get around people that will pray with you and speak life to your situation.

If you close your ears or eyes to those that are put into your life for a purpose, then you can miss the wonderful opportunities and blessings that God has to offer. God may have sent that person in your life to help you or uplift you to a higher level. Cherish and be grateful for those that take time to invest in you. They are investing the brand that is in you and they know you can or will succeed. Most importantly, they have identified gifts, talents, abilities, or skills that you may have that they would like to see you utilize into other people's lives. In Matthew 25:21, "His lord said unto him, well done, thou good and faithful servant: thou has been faithful over a few things, I will make thee ruler over many things: enter thou into the joy of thy lord." It is highly important that you utilize what you have been given because it can eventually diminish if you don't use it.

These good things that our Heavenly Father has given us are for a greater purpose and plan for the kingdom. Take hold of those things that are good and move forward with them. Be thankful and appreciative when you do receive it. If you find yourself focusing on things that have no root or become a hindrance to you moving forward, then you know it is time to let go. In Philippians 3:13-14, "Brethren, I count not myself to have apprehended: but this one thing I do, forgetting those things which are behind, and reaching forth unto those things which are before, I press toward the mark for the prize of the high calling of God in Christ Jesus." Keep your eyes on Jesus! You are beautiful inside and out. Remind yourself that you can do all things through Christ Jesus who strengthens you and that there is power when you believe.

Lastly, go about everyday with the expectancy of something good is going to happen. Keep your eyes on that good thing and look pass the problems that you face in the world. Every problem is an opportunity to present a solution! Every setback is only an opportunity to comeback! Know that you can only change those things that you have control, which starts within you. Keep the drive, energy, passion, love, and joy in all that you do such as accomplishing a set goal or taking a new position in your career path. Also, remember one of the greatest blessings is favor. By having favor, you will see doors open that no man can shut and you will see the mighty hand of God at work in your life. Build relationships and learn from one another. It is amazing that if you are open to receive, you will learn best practices and techniques that have helped others to get where they are. Get out of your comfort zone and explore new ideas. Be who you are and don't go about life trying to impress those around you. In Psalms 139: 14, "I will praise thee; for I am fearfully and wonderfully: marvelous are thy works; and that my soul knoweth right well." You are fearfully and wonderfully made. Invest in yourself and believe in who you are. Give everyday your best! You will make mistakes, but don't let that get you down. Don't let your past mistakes determine your future. Pick yourself back up and try again. You are worthy and valuable. Let your light shine and put a smile on your face. Always remember this, "Believe All Things Are Possible."

Kyle and I have shared with you the importance of believing in who you are…The next step is to be confident in who you are in Christ…Our confidence in the Lord was tested and tried by life's challenges but we continued to cleave to Jesus- the only, true source…Right now, you can put your confidence in the Lord…Start today…

Living With Confidence in the Lord
✝
"Cast not away therefore your confidence, which hath great recompence of reward."
Hebrews 10:35

Do you find yourself dwelling on negative thoughts? Have you been told you are nobody? Are you listening to what other people are saying about you? Do you worry what other people think about you? Stop it right now! You are a child of God! You are the beloved child of God! In Jeremiah 29:11, "For I know the thoughts and plans that I have for you, says the Lord. Thoughts and plans for welfare and peace and not for evil, to give you hope in your final outcome." God loves you for who you are. It doesn't matter what people say about you. You need to know who you are in Christ. Listen to what God says about you. You are fearfully and wonderfully made. In Isaiah 61:10, "I will greatly rejoice in the Lord, my soul shall be joyful in my God; for he hath clothed me with the garments of salvation, he hath covered me with the robe of righteousness, as a bridegroom decketh himself with ornaments, and as a bride adorneth herself with her jewels." You are the righteousness of God. You are a victor not a victim. You are blessed and more than a conqueror. You are everything God designed you to be.

In 2 Timothy 3:17, "That the man of God may be perfect; thoroughly furnished unto all good works." God has equipped and prepared you for what is ahead. He knows everything about you. In Jeremiah 1:5, "Before I formed thee in the belly I knew thee; and before thou camest forth out of the womb I sanctified thee, and I ordained thee a prophet unto the nations." God chose and created you in your mother's womb. He has a purpose and plan for your life. You have been given a life of abundance and overflow of God's blessings. God loves you for who you are.

Lift up your head, child of God! Your victory is here! In Ephesians 3:20, "Now to Him Who, by (in consequence of) the (action of His) power that is at work within us, is able to (carry out His purpose and) do superabundantly, far over and above all that we (dare) ask or think (infinitely beyond our highest prayers, desires, thoughts, hopes, or dreams)." Trust and rely on the Lord. He is your strength! God is able to work through us when we submit our lives to him. We have to surrender and commit our lives to follow Jesus. In 1 John 4:4, "Ye are of God, little children, and have overcome them: because greater is he that is in you, than he that is in the world." Even when you go through storms and battles, know the greater one is in you. Right now, you might be thinking or saying, "Megan, you just don't know what I am going through? If you were in my shoes, then you would think differently?" Get rid of the negative thinking. God promises to turn everything around for your good. In Romans 8:28, "And we know that all things work together for good to them that love God, to them who are called according to his purpose." God will never leave you nor forsake.

Your time is here! God desires to see you succeed victoriously in every area of your life. In 1 Deuteronomy 28:8, "The Lord shall command the blessing upon thee in thy storehouses, and in all that thou settest thine hand unto; and he shall bless thee in the land which the Lord thy God giveth thee." Everything your hand touches shall prosper, multiply, and increase. Your circumstance and situation may look impossible. In Luke 1:37, "For with God nothing shall be impossible." Know with God all things are possible. Let go and hand it over to the Lord. Let him fight your battles and give God all of the glory. It is not over until God says it is over. No matter what you are going through right now, stand strong in the Lord. Stand with confidence and courage. Be of good cheer and know the joy of the Lord is your strength.

When you are facing uncertain circumstances, confess, "I have a mind of Christ. I am confident and strong in the Lord. I am beautiful and mighty in the kingdom of God. I can do all things through Christ who strengthens me." I dare you to be bold and live every moment of your life with expectancy of God's greatness and mercy rising up inside of you. Walk with humility and a humble spirit. Stand with strength and dignity for the kingdom of God. You represent the kingdom of God. You are God's beloved child, so act like it. In1 Peter 2:9, "But ye are a chosen generation, a royal priesthood, a holy nation, a peculiar people; that ye should shew forth the praises of him who hath called you out of darkness into his marvelous light." You are the royal priesthood. Believe in who you are and don't give up on yourself. Refuse to give up and don't settle for less. God has big things in store for you and he only gives you the best. When you are confident in who you are, then other people are confident in you.

Why are you worrying what other people think about you? Walk with confidence and love. Love others unconditionally. For God is love. Lift your head and speak with boldness. Don't have your head down or speak with lack of confidence. Rise up with conviction and confidence in what you say. You are God's chosen ones because he loves you. In Ephesians 6:6-7, "Not with eye service, as men pleasers; but as the servants of Christ, doing the will of God from the heart; with good will doing service, as to the Lord, and not to men." Everything you do, do it wholeheartedly unto the Lord. You serve the kingdom of God. I encourage you to walk in love, develop a Christ-like mindset, and speak faith-filled words like, "I am blessed and loved. I have faith in the kingdom of God. Something good is happening to me, right now. I put my confidence and trust in the kingdom of God. I refuse to give up on myself and God's plan for my life. I have a purpose and God's will be done in my life."

Some people struggle with who they are in Christ. Today, I dare you to be all that God has called you to be. Surrender yourself to Jesus. Commit and dedicate your life to following Jesus. In Joshua 1:15, "Until the Lord have given your brethren rest, as he hath given you, and they also have possessed the land which the Lord your God giveth them; then ye shall return unto the land of your possession, and enjoy it, which Moses the Lord's servant gave you on this side Jordan toward the sunrising." Follow Jesus to the promise land where there is milk and honey running over. Jesus is your prize and reward.

Keep your eyes on Jesus. In Matthew 6:33, "Seek first the kingdom of God and his righteousness; all these other things shall be added unto you." Go to God first in all things and he will direct your path. If you are facing opposition, know God is turning your adversary around for good. God has given you a victorious life!

Next time, someone calls you something you are not or everyone around you is saying you are not going to make it, stand up and declare, "Today is my day. I delight in the Lord. Jesus is my Lord and Savior. I command the enemy to get underneath my feet. Jesus has won my battles and I am a winner in Christ. I walk by faith not by sight. I don't care what it looks like. I have already won, in Jesus Name." Move forward in who you are and remain confident. There is great reward in confidence. You are blessed and you are the upright in God. I dare you to be confident, of good courage, compassionate, loving, caring, gentle, and determined in Christ.

You have identified that God has a purpose, plan, and good things in store for you…Also, you know how vital it is to believe and be confident in who you are in Christ Jesus but we cannot forget the people God has put in our life to help us along the journey…If you have a spouse, children, or loved one that has been there every step of the way, stop and say thank you to that person for never giving up on YOU!…The person I would like to say Thank You, of course, my amazing, strong husband, Kyle Moore…Read my letter of love and gratitude to Kyle…

Love Letter to My Dearest Love
†

"And now abideth faith, hope, charity, these three; but the greatest of these is charity."
1 Corinthians 13:13

November 7, 2012

FROM THE DESK OF MEGAN M. MOORE

Dear Kyle,

This is your special day. The day to always remember with the ones you love. The moment filled with love and laughter. The opportunity to treasure and embrace with loving arms. The day filled with good memories to hold close to your heart. The moment with bursts of joy and thanksgiving.

Sweetheart, I am so thankful that God gave us another day to enjoy and to put in our memory box. He is always good to us. I know you will enjoy this day and you will never forget all the good things God has given us. I asked the Lord what I can give you that will let you know how much I love you. He said, "Prepare a message that is straight from your heart." So, here is the very message from my heart…

I honor and respect you as my husband and my best friend. I thank God for you. You are a gift from above. You are a gift from God. I cherish you and embrace your love. You inspire me to never give up and encourage me to continue on the journey that God is taking me. You love me for who I am and bring out the best in me. You are my spiritual supporter and partner. You inspire me to live every day like it is my last. You lift me up when I down and you catch me when I fall.

Every day, I look up to heaven and thank God for you. He knows I need you and you are part of the Master Plan. God joined us together to carry out his plan and to touch many lives along the way. Our marriage was not an accident; it was a "Miracle" from our Heavenly Father. I thank God for your encouraging words and your heart filled with love. I thank God for teaching you to be the head of our household and the leader of our family that brings glory to him. I adore and admire who you have become in Christ. I thank God for using us to be a blessing to others. You are the Christ-like example for younger men and for our children to come. I love you for who you are. I receive you for who you are.

Honey, I enjoy you and cherish every day he gives us. I thank God for teaching us to walk hand-in-hand together with him as the center. I thank God for his word to help us to forgive and love one another. I thank God for reminding us to pray together when we are faced with an impossible situation.

Finally, I thank God for strengthening our hearts and our marriage. I thank God for his guidance and direction in receiving all that he has in store for us. I love you so much that I know you are a gift from above. I love you forever and for always! I know in my heart that God Never Fails and our Love in him for each other will never fail. LOVE NEVER FAILS…

Blessings and Love,

Your Wife

I have shared with my love for amazing, blessed hubby…In addition, there are some amazing women God has brought into my life to help me be all God has created me to be…Read and capture the beauty of God through these amazing women…

Amazing Women: A Gift from Our Almighty Father
✝
"Who can find a virtuous woman? For her price is far above rubies."
Proverbs 31:10

Right now, look around and identify the amazing women that God has placed in your life. In Matthew 13:45-46, "Again, the kingdom of heaven is like unto a merchant man, seeking goodly pearls; Who, when he had found one pearl of great price, went and sold all that he had, and bought it." Can you say that you have treated them like precious pearls or have you constantly disregarded the beauty that God has planted in their hearts? Are you thanking and admiring God for bringing these amazing women in your life or are you complaining and criticizing them for their past mistakes? By gripping and whining about the little things that don't matter, you are really missing the point!!! God didn't give you these amazing women in your life to take for granted, but to love them for who they are in God's eyes. In God's eyes, they are made perfect through Jesus Christ! They are beautiful and created in the image of God! I definitively say that I have identified and captured the beauty of God through the amazing women in has placed in my path.

It is on my heart to share with you certain amazing women that God had orchestrated and answered years of prayers to bring these uniquely, rare gems in my life…

A greater mother of blended family of ten children, amazing wife to Roy, and a beautiful, inspiring leader, Michelle Boswell is truly a woman sent from Our Heavenly Father into my life and many others. She has encouraged and never given up on me even when other women have thrown in the towels and said enough is enough. Michelle inspires me the way she loves Jesus with all of her heart and gives him first place in her life. She is a woman of integrity, character, stature, professionalism, and strength. Michelle lends her hand to the poor and needy with a cheerful heart. She gives with the expectancy of her provider (Jehovah Jireh) to multiply and prosper every seed released from her precious hands. In John 7:38, "He that believeth on me, as the scripture hath said, out of his belly shall flow river of living water." Michelle blesses others with the word of God that flows like living water from her entire body and the actions of demonstration of faith in Our Heavenly Father. She is well-respected for her commitment and dedication to help women become the women that God designed them to be in him. God has revealed to both of us the greater purpose and plan for our crossed paths. God is a BIG God and he doesn't do anything small or mediocrity. Michelle and I thank God for using us to enhance and build-up the kingdom of God! Everything we say or do is for the edifying of the Body of Christ and to bring our Heavenly Father the glory! Glory be to God!

Next, a fireball of enthusiasm, excitement, energy, and love for our Lord Jesus Christ, Leah Coleman is recognized and captured as an elegant, hand-crafted jewel that sent from above to change generations to generations. In Malachi 3:17, "And they shall be mine, saith the Lord of hosts, in that day when I make up my jewels ; and I will spare them, as a man spareth his own son that serveth him." She is that jewel God designed to call forth and connect his people with their greater purpose in him. Leah is a woman on fire for God and filled with passion to bring the lost souls to Jesus Christ!!! In Philippians 3:14, "I press toward the mark for the prize the high calling of God in Christ Jesus." She inspires and encourages me to keep pressing forward towards the prize of the high calling of Jesus Christ! Leah is well-known for her love for Jesus Christ and to help teenagers to rise in who they are in Jesus and lead their generation. I thank God for bringing a woman of zeal, style, and compassion in my path to direct me straight to the word of God! God divinely orchestrated through several of his people to connect and bring Leah and I together! When God desires for his people to come together in the unity of the body of Christ, he will send his angels to go to work and have us at the right place at the right time. God is faithful and always on time! Trust and wait promptly for his timing to come to pass in your life!

Lastly, a greater friend, mighty prayer partner, and a woman of unfailing love for our Lord Jesus Christ, Micah Winn is truly an angel from our Heavenly Father. It is so amazing how God crossed and connected our paths. She is a woman of truth, honesty, character, compassion, and heart. Micah is admired for her strength in the Lord and her BIG heart to stretch out to those who need God's love. She is well-respected and honored for determination to never give up on what truly matters. Micah encourages and uplifts me to continue reaching out to women who have been led astray or who are hurting from past mistakes. I thank God for pressing it on my heart to stay in contact and to never give up on Micah. God promises he will never leave you nor forsake you! Through the word of God, God has taught Micah and I to be bold, courageous, and confident in our Lord Jesus Christ! He has strengthened and flourished our friendship to inspire others that you can live and enjoy a victorious life in Jesus! In 1 John 5:4, "For whatsoever is born of God overcometh the world; and this is the victory that overcometh the world, even our faith." Micah and I are examples of living the abundant life that Jesus died for us to enjoy.

These are only few of the amazing women God has placed in my life. I am blessed and humbled to have these amazing women in my life! I encourage you to pray and seek God for new, fresh friendships in your life. I know and believe in my heart that God can do the same for you what he has done in my life. In Acts 10:34, " Then Peter opened his mouth, and said, of a truth I perceive that God is no respecter of persons." Ask and watch God bring amazing women in your paths that are faith-filled believers and prayer warriors for the kingdom of God. In the meantime, praise and thank God for his goodness and faithfulness. In Romans 4:21, "And being fully persuaded that, what he had promised, he was able to perform." Stand on God's promises and receive God's promises in your life.

God brings the right people in your life because he loves you…It is up to you to recognize and capture God at work in your life…In order to enjoy those he has brought in your life, you must first the Lord, love yourself, then love others…If not, you will miss out on receiving the fullest of God's blessings…Read and open your heart to God's love…

Love…God Never Fails

†

"The Lord hath appeared of old unto me, saying, Yea, I have loved thee with an everlasting love: therefore with lovingkindness have I drawn thee."
Jeremiah 31:3

The love of our Heavenly Father is unconditional and forgiving. He is our true Source. Our Heavenly Father is the only one we are to seek ever second, every minute, every day, and every moment of our lives. Love never fails. God never fails. We wait for God, but why? He is already there! In Romans 8:31, "What shall we then say to these things? If God be for us, who can be against us?" God is for and with us! He is waiting for us to move forward with confidence and faith. In Hebrews 11:6, "But without faith it is impossible to please him; for he that come to God must believe that he is, and that he is a rewarder of them that diligently seek him." He needs us to trust him. God loves us! We have to identify who God really is. He desires and longs for us to have an intimate, personal relationship with him.

God is calling out to us and has chosen us to fulfill his purpose. He needs us to be strong and courageous in the kingdom of God. We need to be willing to give ourselves to God so that he can use us to carry out his plan. His plan is to bless us, prosper us, and reward us for our diligence. Do you know that God is true to his word? In Isaiah 55:11, "So shall my word be that goeth forth out of my mouth; it shall not return unto me void, but it shall accomplish that which I please, and it shall prosper in the thing whereto I sent it." His word does not return void. In Romans 4:20-21, "He staggered not at the promise of God through unbelief; but was strong in faith, giving glory to God; And being fully persuaded that, what he had promised, he was able also to perform." He is faithful to fulfill his promises in our life. Stand and meditate on God's promises. Know and believe in your heart that God's promises shall come to pass in your life. He loves you! God has good things in store for us. He only gives his beloved children the best of the best.

Through life, we struggle with our feelings, emotions, and moods. We have to put that aside and be led by the Holy Spirit so that we can see what is out in front of us. Sometimes we can miss it, but there are times when God gives us another opportunity. As long as we seek and serve him, we can see the miracles that are working in our lives and those around us. In Matthew 6:33, "Seek first the kingdom of God and his righteousness; all these other things will be added unto to us." It is very important that we go to God's word so that we can see and hear him.

He speaks through his word. In John 16:13, "Howbeit when he, the Spirit of truth, is come, he will guide you into all truth; for he shall not speak of himself; but whatsoever he shall hear, that shall he speak; and he will shew you things to come." His word is the truth and the truth makes us free. God even speaks to us in different ways. For example, I started a business, God-given business, and I began to experience challenges. I went before God and asked for help and for direction. He heard my cry and sent a woman of God. A woman who is confident in who she is in Christ. A woman that is courageous with style, on fire for God, and anointed with the Holy Ghost. A woman that is blessed by the grace of God and passionate to serve the kingdom of God. When she spoke, it was God speaking directly to me. Everything I needed to hear, he spoke through this woman. The Lord spoke through her to remind me to put him first and his name above all names. In Matthew 6:33, "But seek ye first the kingdom of God, and his righteousness; and all these things shall be added unto you." God comes first then family then church then mission work. We have to give our whole heart to God.

On that day, I experienced the spirit of revelation. God grabbed my attention and revealed his never-ending love. God used my amazing, dearest friend to capture my focus and remind me to put him first in everything, EVERYTHING! After I encountered a manifestation of the Lord's presence, I lifted my eyes and hands to worship him.

Open your mouth and praise him. He is worthy of your praises…

"I glorify and praise you, Heavenly Father! I magnify your name. You are my Daddy! You are already there! In Romans 8:31, "What shall we then say to these things? If God be for us, who can be against us?" Jesus, you are in us and with us. You comfort us, secure us, and protect us from harm. God, you love us because we are your children. I thank you for all the good things in my life. You have rescued, carried, and healed me from my troubles. God, you love us and God, you are love. I rejoice and honor you, Heavenly Father! You are faithful. I am who I am in Christ Jesus. You promises to never leave me nor forsake me. I walk in your love. For God, you are love!"

God loves you as much as he loves Jesus. He honors you because you have Jesus as your Lord and Savior. Jesus is Lord of Lords and King of Kings. We are to go though Jesus to reach the Father. God is our Daddy and our Father. We are his Beloved children. In John 3:16, "For God so loved the world that he gave us his begotten Son, whosoever believes in him shall not perish, but have everlasting life." God loves us because he loves us. He loves us no matter what. God is who he says he is. In Exodus 3:14, "And God said unto Moses, I M THAT I AM; and he said, Thus shalt thou say unto the children of Israel, I AM hath sent me unto you." Believe in your Heavenly Father and know that he loves you. You are who you are in Christ. When you accepted Jesus as your Lord and Savior, you became a new creature and you are born again child of God. You are his child and he loves you so much. God's love is unconditional and he is love. Love is God. You are who God says you are.

Walk in the Holy Spirit so you can hear the Father's voice. Hearken to the voice of Father. He has a purpose and plan for your life. He loves you and needs you to be obedient. Be obedient and listen to his instructions. In John 10:10, "The thief is out to steal, kill, and destroy, but Jesus came so that we would have life, and have life more abundantly." Lift your eyes to your Daddy. In Romans 8:15, "For ye have not received the spirit of bondage again to fear; but ye have received the spirit of adoption, whereby we cry, Abba, father." He is the one who you need. Believe that you are his and be loved. Jesus has opened his arms to comfort you and embrace you with the love of God. He is ready to lead you to the promise land. Walk in the light for God is light. Follow him to the promise land for there is milk and honey. Your Daddy will show you those things that are before you. In Psalms 46:10, "Be still, and know that I am God; I will be exalted among the heathen, I will be exalted in the earth." Be still and listen. The promise land is his kingdom and in his kingdom there is riches and honor.

Believe unto your Heavenly Father and he will bless you. He has made you a blessing to be a blessing. God loves you so much. Love never fails and God never fails. In Proverbs 22:17, "Bow down thine ear, and hear the words of the wise, and apply thine heart unto my knowledge." Open your ears to hear and open your eyes to see and you shall understand with your heart. For God have good things in store for you. His plan is to excel, prosper, and bless you. In Isaiah 55:8-9, "For my thoughts are not your thoughts, neither are your ways my ways, saith the Lord. For as the heavens are higher than the earth, so are my ways higher than your ways, and my thoughts than your thoughts." Our Daddy loves us. He is faithful and true to his word. Speak and walk in the love of God. In Ephesians 3:17, "That Christ may dwell in your hearts by faith; that you, being rooted and grounded in love..." For love casts out fear and is not touchy. Love is kind and not fretful. Love envies not and is not puffed. Love never fails. Know your Father for he is love. By knowing the love of God, you can let his light shine and walk in the love. Renew your mind day by day so that his light can shine. In him lies the blessing. The blessing of Abraham is upon me and my household. Be fruitful, multiply, replenish, and subdue it. You have dominion over this earth.

By knowing your Father and speaking the blessing, you can receive those good things that are in his kingdom. He loves you and he blesses you for your obedience. We are to speak and walk in the blessing. The blessing is in the kingdom of God. His kingdom operates under the blessing of the law. You are blessed and loved. Stand strong in the Lord. The joy of the Lord is your strength. Be joyful and take the blessing. Take ownership of the blessing and receive it. The blessing is yours; claim it, have it, and forgive ought against any. You are blessed.

You are the apple of God's eye. He has you in the palm of his hand. Confess aloud,

"I am blessed, I am blessed, and I am blessed." He loves me so much. Be loved.

Stop struggling to beloved. Just be loved. Let him love you.

Hopefully by now, you know God loves you as much as he loves Jesus... Next, reflect on how beautiful you are in him and how amazing God is to you...You are made for so much more...Kyle and I encourage you to admire how good God truly is...

The Beauty of His Kingdom
†
"Honour and majesty are before him: strength and beauty are in his sanctuary."
Psalm 96:6

Do you recognize and capture the beauty of his majesty? Do you know how amazing our Heavenly Father really is? Everything we face, God turns it around for our good. He only gives us good gifts. Our Father is always there for us. We are never alone. Even when we feel like we are alone, he is there. No matter what we go through in life, he gives us comfort and peace. Jesus is the Prince of Peace. In Matthew 11:28, "For those who are heavy laden or labor, I will give you rest."

God is for us and with us. I know he is fighting my battles and working on my behalf. In Corinthians 4:18, "While we look not at the things which are seen, but at the things which are not seen; for the things which are seen are temporal; but the things which are not seen are eternal." We are to walk by faith, not by sight. Have faith in him. We are to put our trust and confidence in God. Our Father rewards those who diligently seek him. The greatest reward is following Jesus and being obedient to his voice. When he puts it on your heart to reach out to a friend, act on it. There is a purpose and beauty behind his word. We may not understand, but there are some things we just don't need to know. Take time to listen and follow him.

Today, I saw the hand of God at work in my life. There is so much beauty in his Name. He shared with me the beauty of his kingdom. I could feel his presence and hear his voice so clearly. God is moving me to a higher level in his kingdom. I know it and it is so beautiful. It is so amazing to know and to see his hand at work. I have developed and found a deeper part of my relationship with God. He is using me to reach and help others who are finding who they are in Christ.

Every day, I identify the blessings and miracles of God. He is directing me to minister and bless those who are hopeless or brokenhearted. Especially, women who are troubled, confused, and held captive by the enemy. God is leading me to inspire and empower women by sharing my testimony. He is speaking to me that it is time and I know it is happening in his timing. There is power in our testimonies and he wants us to use them for his glory. Everything we do is unto our God and it is for him to receive the glory. I believe our testimonies will lead souls to Jesus Christ and the ones who have drifted away from him will come back.

We are nothing without God. We need him and all of him. God is in us and he has given us Jesus. God loves us as much as he loves Jesus. He created us in his image and chose us because he loves us. According to Genesis 1, "God created man and woman in his image." We are fearfully and wonderfully made. We are worthy and valuable. We are who he is and he is in us. We are his children and he wants to bless us with good things. Everything is for him and to enhance his kingdom. In his kingdom there are riches and honor. He has given it to us. We have to know what is his is ours.

God has given us everything we need to carry out his purpose and plan for our lives. His beauty is to enrich and strengthen us to see his will done. He is bringing the right people and tools in our path to see his plan carried through. God gives us the best and only the best. I give him glory and praise. I magnify and lift up his Name. We serve a real and AWESOME God!

I thank him every day for the many blessings in my life. I would not be here and as strong as I am, if it wasn't for the grace of God. He has made me into a strong, confident, and bold woman. Every morning, I wake up and thank him for being alive and ask him to take my life and do something with it. I follow and surrender myself to Jesus. I only do what my Father does and say what he says. I commit my life to serve his kingdom where there is beauty, mercy, goodness, and joy. I bless his Name, which is above all Names. Thank you God for the amazing people in my life and for reminding me that I am who I am in Christ Jesus.

You have captured and recognized how beautiful you are in Christ Jesus but what are you speaking over yourself and your family...Your words have power...They either speak life or death...Kyle and I have learned the power of our tongue...We decided to speak life and blessing...Read and open your mind to a new way of thinking...

The Blessing of Abraham
†
"Blessed is the man that trusteth in the Lord, and whose hope the Lord is."
Jeremiah 17:7

We are the seed of Abraham and the righteousness of God. We are blessed and made a blessing to be a blessing to others. In Galatians 3:13-14, "Christ has redeemed us from the curse of the law, being made a curse for us: for it is written, Cursed is every one that hang on a tree: That the blessing of Abraham might come on the Gentiles through Jesus Christ; that we might receive the promise of the Spirit through." We have been set free and redeemed from the curse of the law. Jesus Christ has redeemed us from the curse at Calvary. He borne our sicknesses, diseases, and illnesses to the Cross. He nailed them to the Cross. Jesus took our sins to the Cross, so that we would be forgiven. We are forgiven and cleansed through the blood of Jesus Christ. Jesus did it all for us at Calvary. It is finished and done.

Are you speaking the blessing or the curse over your family? In Galatians 3:29, "And if you be Christ's, then are you Abraham's seed, and heirs according to the promise." We are Abraham's seed and joint heirs with Christ. We are the royal priesthood and seated in heavenly places with our Father. We are blessed to be a blessing. Before you speak, think about what you are about to say. According to Proverbs 18:21, "Death and life are in the power of the tongue: and they that love it shall eat the fruit thereof." What you say is what you have. Are you speaking increase, abundance, overflow, favor, prosperity, and blessing over you and your household? In Joshua 24:15, "Are for me and my household, we shall serve the Lord all the days of our lives." We are the body of Christ and clothed with the robe of righteousness. We blessed, wise, wealthy, and in good health. Speak after me, "I am blessed, wise, wealthy, and in good health." Right now, begin to mediate on those words. Everyday confess those words and share them with others. Put the word of God in your eyes, ears, and mouth. When you mediate on his word, then your mind and heart becomes renewed and restored.

Are you barely getting by and wondering how you are going to pay your next bill? Get in the word of God and stand on his word. Stand on scriptures for prosperity and blessing. Find out what God says about living in lack. He is our source and provider. He is a more than enough God. We are living in the land of more than enough. When Jesus redeemed us from the curse at Calvary, he released blessing, increase, abundance, and overflow into our lives. In Psalm 103:15, "As for man, his days are as grass: as a flower of the field, so he flourish." We are flourishing and overflowing in the house of our Lord. We are blessed and we have a rich, rich Daddy. Stop complaining, whining, and begging God to get you out of your messed up financial situation. Find out what the word of God has to say about your situation. Jesus is the answer to the problem. Stop taking ownership of the problem and stop telling your friends and family about the issue. Start confessing with your mouth, "I am the blessed child of God. My Daddy is rich, rich. The blessing of Abraham is upon me and my household. Everything my hand touches shall prosper, increase, and multiply. I walk by faith not by sight. My checking and savings account are overflowing. Money come into me, now. I am blessed going in and coming out. I am blessed in the field and the city. My basket and storehouse are blessed. I receive everything that you have in store for me. I take it, receive it, and claim it by faith, In Jesus Name, Amen." God wants his children to prosper and increase. Ask the Lord what he has you to do. He may have you bless someone in need or minister to someone about financial prosperity. Get in the word of God and stay in the word. Keep your feet planted in the word of God and don't even think about putting your feet in the world's system.

Who are you surrounding yourself with? Are you surrounding yourself with people who believe in the world's system of meeting their own needs? Or people who trust in God for their income? Pray and ask the Lord to put Christian people in your path. Associate and surround yourself with people that put God first and that are going to pray with you. Ask God to remove those who are a hindrance to you moving forward and that are bringing you down. Ask the Lord to bring people in your path that will help you grow and develop in word of God. Keep in mind that the influence in your life is who you will become. Be watchful and alert in who you let in your life. Guard your heart and mind from negativity. Speak blessing over everyone you come into contact with. The blessing flows unto everything that we touch and everything that pertains to us.

Our Daddy longs for us to enjoy the blessings and opportunities that he gives us. He loves you so much. He loves all of us. His love is unconditional and never failing. In 1 Corinthians 13:8, "Love never fails…" God never fails and he is faithful and true to his word. Never settle for less and let God take you to higher level. A higher level of blessings, promotion, opportunities, and favor from God. Keep your eyes fixed on the Lord. Jesus is the way and he will keep you on the right path. When you begin to steer off course, ask the Lord to get you back on the right track. Maintain your focus on our King and refuse to never give up. Your breakthrough is here. Speak the blessing of Abraham over you and your household. We are set free in Christ Jesus and we are blessed to be a blessing.

Now, you understand the power of your tongue...Even when you going through a Huge storm, your tongue has power to speak to it...The words you speak will either keep you where you are at or take you to the next BIG opportunity...Kyle and I have learned to hold onto the word of God...Read and be inspired to not talk about the storm but talk to the storm...

Storms Bring a Flood of Opportunities

✝

"And he arose, and rebuked the wind, and said unto the sea, Peace, be still. And the wind ceased, and there was a great calm. And he said unto them, why are you so fearful? how is it that you have no faith?"
Mark 4:39-40

You might often wonder why are you facing storms and why does it seem that everything is starting to crumble at your feet? God never said that life was going to be easy. When you accepted Jesus in your heart, you became a new creature. A new man in Christ means old things have passed and all things have become new. By dedicating your life to Christ meant that you are willing to go through times of troubles and struggles. Even though you go through times of restlessness, trust in the Lord with all of your heart and rest yourself in the Lord. Do not let the times of troubles or struggles defeat you. The Devil will try to pull you down, but you have to know that you have authority over Devil. Denounce the past and everything the Devil stands on. You are an over comer of all obstacles. You are a victor and not a victim. You are more than a conqueror.

No matter what you face in life, God will never leave you nor forsake you. God loves you and his love is unconditional. God's word contains everything you need to get through storms, outlines his purpose for your life, and gives you guidance to having a victorious life. If you have Jesus in your heart, then you will have the desire to seek God's word. Before you accepted Jesus as your Lord and Savior, do you remember how lost you were with no sense of direction and how you were living in darkness? Jesus is the answer to every situation and he is longs for you to reach out to him. He needs you to put him first. Matthew 6:33 says, "Seek first the kingdom of God and his righteousness; all these things will be added unto you." In order to put God first, you have to trust him and have faith in his word. Faith comes from hearing the word, hearing the word of God. You have to activate your faith with actions and be doers of the word.

Even though you may be dealing with a circumstance that seems impossible, you have to understand that your faith determines your outcome. Also, you have to stand strong in your faith because the Devil works hard to try to weaken it. Believe God with your whole heart and give yourself to the Lord. Your faith in God indicates that no matter what you go through life, you will follow and serve his kingdom. Do not let the world's cares bring you to a place of defeat, discouragement, and weary. Cast all of your cares unto the Lord and know the love of Jesus Christ. His love for you will never change. God is the same yesterday, today, and tomorrow. God has the best in store for you and unexpected explosive blessings are coming your way. Jesus is the way, the truth, and the life. Love God with all of your heart. You are nothing without God. God made you who you are and created you to be who you are in Christ. Be blessed. Be loved.

Today is your day…Look at your storm and see yourself passing through it as a victor or more than an over comer…Don't remain but trust God to carry you through it…Over the years, Kyle and I have realized that you cannot put your trust in man but only the true helper-Jesus…Continue to read and make a decision to trust God…

Trust In the Lord
†
"Trust in the Lord with all thine heart; and lean not unto thine own understanding."
Proverbs 3:5

Do you find yourself searching for answers? Are you trying to make it in your own strength? Do you go to bed at night and wonder about tomorrow? It says in Matthew 6:34, "So do not worry or be anxious about tomorrow, for tomorrow will have worries and anxieties of its own. Sufficient for each day is its own trouble." Are you really trusting God or are you worrying about what only God can control? Why are you spending your life with anger, unforgiveness, resentment, and worry? Why not spend your life trusting your Heavenly Father? In Proverbs 3:5, "Lean on, trust in, and be confident in the Lord with all your heart and mind and do not rely on your own insight or understanding." It is amazing, when you trust God; he immediately goes to work on your behalf. He lines up the right people in your path and directs your steps to fulfilling his plan for your life.

According to Proverbs 3:6, "In all your ways know, recognize, and acknowledge him, and he will direct and make straight and plain your paths." Put God first and pray over everything, EVERYTHING! He is faithful and true to his word. Man has a hard time keeping their promises, but God always fulfill his promises. In Matthew 6:33, "But seek (aim at and strive after) first of all His kingdom and His righteousness (His way of doing and being right), and then all these things taken together will be given you besides. Seek his ways and his thoughts.

According to Isaiah 26:4, "So trust in the Lord (commit yourself to Him, lean on Him, hope confidently in Him) forever; for the Lord God is an everlasting Rock (the Rock of Ages)." Right now, you may be facing an impossible situation, or a rebellious child, or a struggling marriage, or a loved one fighting for their life. Get in the word and say, "Father, I trust you! I will not say anything contrary to the word of God. I will only speak your word. Jesus, you are the answer. I surrender myself to you. I turn over my marriage, finances, children, relationships, career, business, and family over to you. I turn everything over to you. I command Satan to take his hands off of everything that pertains to me and my household. In Joshua 24:15, "As for me and my household, we will serve the Lord all of the days of our life." I plead the blood of Jesus over the situation, my children, my marriage, my family, finances, and everything connected to me and my household. In Jesus Name, Amen." Do not let up. Do not be a lazy and do not sit around whining about what God can only change. Say, "I put my trust in you, God. I do not put my trust in man. I trust you, Father."

God loves you deeply and unconditionally. He has given you Jesus; his precious gift from Heaven to you. Never take for granted for what Christ did for you and me at Cavalry. Jesus borne our sicknesses and diseases and nailed them to the Cross. He was wounded for our transgressions and bruised for your iniquities. He done it all for us and he finished it at Cavalry. Jesus fought every battle and he made the sacrifice for our sins. We are forgiven and free in Christ. Jesus redeemed us from the curse and released abundance into our lives. So, next time the enemy throws an evil word or thought at you, say, "I am forgiven. I trust God. I believe the Lord." When you submit and trust God, then the enemy has no other choice, but to flee. In James 4:7, "So be subject to God. Resist the devil (stand firm against him), and he will flee from you." Stand strong in the Lord. Do not be afraid or fearful. In 1 Timothy 1:7, "For God did not give us a spirit of timidity (of cowardice, of craven and cringing and fawning fear), but (he has given us a spirit) of power and of love and of calm and well-balanced mind and discipline and self-control." Walk by faith and trust God for good things to happen in your life. For God only gives us good things to enjoy. In Romans 8:28, "And we know that all things work together for good to them that love God, to them who are called according to his purpose." Only good gifts come from above.

Today, make the commitment to stay focused on the Lord. Do not waste your life trying to figure everything out. Even if you think you have it figured out, you really don't. God is our helper and only he knows the plans for our life. He created us in his image and chose us to fulfill his purpose. Walk with confidence and courage in the Lord. Trust the Lord with all of your heart and mind. He has the best in store for you and your family. Keep standing on the word of God and keep on believing in the Lord. In due time, whatever you believe God for, according to his will, shall come to pass. When the enemy comes at you with, "It is not going to work out; it will never happen; give up because it's over." You lift your eyes up to Heaven and say, "It is written, Our Father who is in heaven, hallowed be your name, your kingdom come. Your will be done (held holy and revered) on earth as it is in heaven." Stay focused on God and everything is going to be al-right!

By trusting God, he can shape and mold you into a beautiful masterpiece… God has taken my life and transformed it into a reflection of his glory… I did not have a mother figure to teach me how to be a woman of God or to be a helper meet to my husband or to be a mother… I thank God for teaching me through his word in how to be a woman of God, a sweet, gentle helper meet to my husband, and soon-to-be mother to our children… If you are woman reading this book, I encourage you to ask God to do the same for you… Continue to read and this piece will help you to be a Proverbs 31 woman…

Victorious Women Step Forward

✝

"Give her of the fruit of her hands; and let her own works praise her in the gates."
Proverbs 31:31

You are a woman of fire and energy from within. Be the one who is confident in you. Let nobody tell you otherwise. Invest in who you are and use your God-given gifts, talents, and abilities. God gave you everything you need to carry out his plan. You are fearfully and wonderfully-made. You are a victor not a victim. You are worthy and valuable. You are God's jewel. He has placed you in the palm of his hand. You are the key to unlocking the treasure. It is within you. Do you often find yourself searching for those hidden opportunities? God has planted them in you. Take a look at where you are standing and you will find it.

You have an amazing Father! He knows everything about and he knows your every move. God understands who you are because he is in you and with you. He loves you no matter what. His love is unconditional and ever-lasting. In 1 Corinthians 13, "...Love Never Fails." God is love and love is God. Love one another as Jesus loves you. Be rooted and grounded in love. Know who God is, walk in his love, and let his light shine. He created and chose you because he loves you. God has a specific purpose and plan for your life.

According to Proverbs 31:10, "She is far more precious than jewels and her value is far above rubies or pearls." You are a beautiful and unique woman of God. He admires and adores the beauty of his children. In Proverbs 31:25, "Strength and dignity are her clothing and her position is strong and secure; she rejoices over the future..." Your strength and confidence is in the Lord. Put your trust in his kingdom. You have a mind of Christ. Confess, "I have a mind of Christ," with boldness and truthfulness. God made you an image of him.

He made you in the image of Jesus and in him there is blessing. When you have the blessing of Abraham, then you receive a victorious life with overflow and abundance. It has been given to us. All you have to do is take it and receive it and know it is yours. When you ask for Godly wisdom and knowledge, then it shall be given unto you. In Proverbs 31:26, "She opens her mouth in skillful and godly Wisdom, and on her tongue is the law of kindness (giving counsel and instruction)." Be bold and courageous in the kingdom of God. Stand strong in the Lord and speak with boldness before the throne of God. By his grace (unmerited favor or Lord's strength), we capture the majesty of his beauty. Our beauty is from him. Give your Father in Heaven the glory. He is an AWESOME and VICTORIOUS God!

According to Proverbs 31:30, "Charm and grace are deceptive, and beauty is vain (because it is not lasting), but a woman who reverently and worshipfully fears the Lord, she shall be praised!" True beauty is the honor and fear for the Lord. Be obedient woman of God! God rewards those who diligently seek him and hearken to his voice. Make a commitment and dedication today to follow Jesus. Surrender yourself to JESUS! Speak and claim over you and your household the blessing and the victorious life. You have what you say! You are God's children and he loves you so much! Spend time with God and invest in you! Encourage, Inspire, Empower, and Uplift your sisters in Christ! Believe in who you are and Believe ALL Things Are Possible! Celebrate and Rejoice the Victorious Woman, in YOU!

You are the person God created you to be…Your life is full of decisions and choices but sometimes we get so strapped down in the busyness that we miss out in praising God… Take this moment to give praises and thanksgivings to our Lord and Savior, Jesus Christ…

Worship for the King

†

"Sing unto the Lord, bless his name; shew forth his salvation from day to day."
Psalm 96:2

I added this piece of writing to share with you that my faith walk has not been easy… One day, I fell to my knees with desperation and emptiness to our Lord and Savior, Jesus… I believe every believer of the word of God comes to a fork in the road where they fall to their knees to signify to Jesus, "I can't do this without you…" When I fell to my knees, I knew that I could no longer hold back what I was feeling and experiencing at that very moment… Tears and words exploded out of me like an erupting volcano… When I fully let go and let God take the wheel, I was set free and I strengthened by his healing power…Let this writing inspire and encourage you to look within…Lift up your hands or fall to knees…Do what you need to do to worship our King…

God you know everything, EVERYTHING about me. When I am weak, you are STRONG. Right now, Lord I am looking to you for the right words to speak. I need you, Lord. My heart cries out for you. I am longing for you. I trust you Lord with all of my heart. I am yours, Lord. I give all of me to you. I love you Lord. I am weeping inside. I am trying to look strong, but I know I need your strength. I am sitting right here seeking for you. I know you are here. I want you Lord! I need you Lord! What is happening to me, Lord? I know you know my weaknesses and my pain. I am trembling at your feet, Lord! You are my EVERYTHING, Lord! Your love is unconditional, Lord. You know everything about me. You know the obstacles and storms I am going through, but I know you are with me. You promise to never leave me nor forsake me. Jesus, you are the answer and solution to the impossible circumstances and situations. I need you, Jesus. Jesus, I love you! I know you love me so much. I am only here today because of you, Lord. No matter what I am feeling, I know you are strengthening me in you.

My value and worth is in you, Lord! Jesus you are so beautiful and powerful. You are my Rock and Strong tower. You are my refugee and buckler! I exalt your Name, Jesus! Your name is above every name, Jesus! I lift your name, Jesus above every Name! I magnify you Jesus! I worship you Father! I give you the glory, Father for all the good things in my LIFE. I know only good things come from you, Father! You are my helper, deliverer, advocate, and counselor! Jesus you are the prince of peace! You are who you say you are! Jesus you are the light! Jesus you are so precious to me! Thank you for taking our sins to the Cross! I give my life to you, Jesus! I turn my marriage, relationships, finances, family, career, health, and household over to you! I give it to you! It is yours! I refuse to hold to the cares of this world! I life this load off of my shoulders and hand it over to you! You know my pain and the struggles I face, but I know you are carrying me. I see you, Jesus! Your arms are opened wide for me. I come to you, Jesus! I run to you, Jesus! I embrace you, Jesus! I feel your loving arms wrapped around me! Your touch is unconditional, refreshing, and rejuvenating! Oh, how beautiful you are, Jesus! Your touch heals and repairs the brokenness in me! Your presence restores me in you! Jesus, you are always here! Even when I feel alone, you are always here for me! Jesus, your presence is so magnificent and beautiful!

Your light is filled with warmth and comfort! Your love is who you are! Jesus, you are mighty and wonderful! I follow you, Jesus! I follow you, Jesus! I will never leave your side! I come to you, Jesus! I am yours, Jesus! I feel your hand in mine, Jesus! I know you are guiding and directing my steps! Oh, I love you, Jesus! I know where you are taking is so amazing and beautiful! You are taking me to the promise land where there is milk and honey running over! A place where there is overflow and abundance! I trust you Lord even though I don't understand! I am yours, Jesus! I love you, Jesus! Jesus, you walk with me through the fire! You are my healer! Jesus, you are all I need! I believe in you, Jesus! I trust you, Jesus! Where I am going, you are with me! You are my Redeemer! I surrender myself to you, Jesus! I give myself to you for you to use me to carry out your purpose! Take my life and do something with it! I am yours, Jesus!

You hold my life in my hand! I am the apple of your eye! I believe you are who you say you are! I come to you, Jesus! I run to you, Jesus! I long for you, Jesus! I hunger and thirst for your word, Father! I praise you, Jesus! I worship you, Jesus! I lift your name above every name! You are so holy! I give you thanksgiving! Jesus, you are Lord and Savior over my Life! Jesus, you are Lord of Lords and King of Kings! Jesus, you are my everything! Oh, how I adore you! I admire you, Jesus! I commit and dedicate my life to follow you, Jesus! I follow you, Jesus! My value and worth is you, Jesus!

I forsake those things that are not of you, Father! Shine light on those areas that are dark! Your word is the lamp of my feet! You are mighty and powerful! You are the Almighty, God! I rest in you, Jesus! You are my strengthener! You are my healer! You are more than enough! You more than what I need! You are everything I need and want! I run to you, Jesus! I trust in you! I believe in you, Jesus! I believe you are all that I need! I believe you aremy portion! Jesus, you are all that I need! Nothing is impossible with you! I believe all things are possible with you, Jesus! You hold my life in your hand! You are my Savior and my

Deliverer! You are who you say you are! You are my hero! Jesus, you are real! Jesus, you are alive in me! I am at your feet, Jesus! I pour my heart at your feet! I know I am weak! Your joy is my strength! I lift my eyes to you, Jesus! My eyes are fixed on you, Jesus! My eyes are locked on you, Jesus! I am here, Jesus! I cannot do this in my own strength or works! I am forever yours! I give it all to you, Jesus! I cast my burdens unto you, Jesus! I will always be yours! My hands are yours! My feet are yours! My body is yours! My household is yours! I serve you, Lord! I am here to know more of you! I rest in your presence! I know there is refuge and peace in your presence! Oh, how beautiful you are, Jesus! I will rest in you, Jesus! I refuse to try to figure it out! I am here to hear from you, Father! I come to you, Jesus! My troubles are yours! You are my deliverer! I am a new creation in you! My life is new in you, Jesus! I look to you Jesus! My eyes are yours! When I look at my eyes, I see you Jesus! I am a reflection of you, Jesus! I am forgiven in you, Jesus! I am made whole in you! I love you, Jesus! Oh, how your love is overflowing and everlasting! Your love never fails!

You have made a way for me in your presence! Your presence is right here! In the secret place is where I find you! I seek for you and you are always there! When I feel empty inside, you come in and fill me with all of you! You fill me with you! Oh, how you love us so much! Your loving arms are wrapped around me! We are your children and how you love us so much! We are your beloved children! Thank you, Jesus! Thank you, Jesus! Oh, how you love us so much! Jesus, you love us so much! Yes, you love us so much! You are our prize and our reward! Oh, how you love us, Jesus! Jesus you love us so much! There is nothing like your love! You know EVERYTHING about me! Oh, you love us so much, Jesus! I give you praise and thanksgiving! Jesus, I am yours!

I run to you, Jesus! I am hurting and aching inside! I am going through overwhelming emotions! It seems like everything is falling apart, but I know you here! I feel your loving arms wrapped around me. Your touch reminds me that I am not alone! Your presence reminds me that you are in control! I feel you wiping the tears from my face! I am trembling and falling apart inside, but you call out my name! You speak soft words to my heart! Your words are the very words my heart is searching for! You remind me to be still in you! My heart is steady in you! My body rests in your hands! I feel you carrying and raising me to a higher place in you! Oh, Lord, how you know the right words to speak to me! Jesus, I consume all of you! I see you, Jesus!

Even my weakest days, I feel you closer than ever before! You breathe your word into my spirit! In your presence, I am strong, confident, and courageous! I lift my eyes and head to you, Jesus! My heart belongs to you, Jesus! I love you, Jesus! Show me your mercy and goodness! I am yours! I praise you, Jesus! Jesus, you are Risen! You are my Savior and Lord! I will rise to praise you, Jesus! I give you the glory! I glorify you, Jesus! I magnify and lift you up, Jesus! You are worthy for our praises! I love you, Jesus! Hallelujah, Hallelujah! Oh, how I adore and admire you, Jesus! I cry out to you, Jesus! I use to live alone, but now I have you Jesus! Oh, Jesus, how precious you are! I was lost, now I am found in you! I was dead, now I am alive in you! Oh, Jesus, how you care so much for me! Jesus, you love us so much! Thank you, Jesus! Thank you, Jesus!

I am on my knees and there you are! You are always are time! You are so faithful! I open my eyes to you, Jesus! When I open my eyes, I see you! When I rest, you steady and stable my body in you! When I wake up, there you are to use me! When I cry, you are there to wipe my tears! When I tremble to my knees, you lift my head to you! When I am weak, you are there to strengthen me in you! You are my loving God and you are true to your word! You are AWESOME and POWERFUL! Thank you Jesus! You are my healer, restorer, and deliverer! You are for me and with me! You promise to never leave me nor forsake me! Thank you your name, Jesus! Thank you for the power in the name of Jesus! Your blood cleanses me! I am set free in you! I can see in you! I am healed in your Name! Oh, how great you are, Jesus!

My chains are broken and I am set free in you! I am no longer held captive! I can fly with you, Jesus! I soar with you, Jesus! I can be who I am in you! My freedom is you, Jesus! Thank you, Jesus! You are real and powerful! I will bless your name, Jesus! I bless you, Lord! Thank you, Jesus! I worship you and it is all about you, Jesus! It was always about you, Jesus! Everything I do is about you! Thank you Jesus! Thank you, Jesus! I open my heart to you, Jesus! I give my heart to you, Jesus! I have walked through the fire with you, Jesus! I am all yours, Jesus! Carry me away, Jesus! You are my every day, every way, and everything! You are all that I need! You are my peace! You are my refuge! You are my strength! You are my all! Thank you, Jesus!

Once you have worshipped and poured your heart out to the King, remain still and invite Jesus to fill you up with the fruit of the Spirit… Kyle and I have celebrated and made time to rest in the presence of the Lord… You and your family can experience the presence of Jesus in your home…

Dwelling In the Secret Place
†
"He that dwelleth in the secret place of the most High shall abide under the shadow of the Almighty."
Psalm 91: 1

Who do you look for protection and security? Who do call upon when you are in trouble? Do you automatically pick up the phone and start dialing a family member or friend's number? Who do you rely on for the answers to your problems? All of these questions relate to your relationship with God. Instead of looking to man, focus your attention towards your one and only help – Jesus! We are nothing without Jesus! Do you remember how you were lost and dead before you accepted Jesus as your Lord and Savior? He is our resting place and he is the Prince of Peace. Our Father gave us Jesus, so our sins would be forgiven and for us to live under the blessing of Abraham. Jesus had borne our sorrows and grief. He nailed them to the cross. He was bruised for our iniquities. God loves each one of us. He is no respecter of persons. God expects us to put him first in all that we do, say, or think. Even when we don't feel like spending time in the word, it is very essential to deepen our relationship with God. Go to that secret place or that hiding place and speak to your Father. He longs and waits for you to come to him.

According to Psalm 91:1-2, "He who dwells in the secret place of the Most High shall remain stable and fixed under the shadow of the Almighty (whose power no foe can withstand). I will say of the Lord, he is our Refuge and my Fortress, my God; on Him I lean and rely, and in Him I (confidently) trust!" We are to endure or continue to spend time with God in that secret place. Go where it is just you and him. When you are in that secret place, you abide under the shadow of the Almighty. His power is upon you and working through you. You will receive his anointing. When you are in his presence, then you have entered the throne of grace. Speak to God about the things you know only he can change. Cast all your cares upon him. God is the only person who can take care of an impossible situation. In Mark 10:27, "Jesus looking upon them said, "With men it is impossible, but not with God; for with God all things are possible." With God nothing is impossible. Every morning wake up and spend time with God first. Put God first in all things. When you put him first in your day, relationships, work, marriage, decisions, and situations, then you have his covering upon you. When you come in the Name of Jesus, anything you ask for, believe you have received by faith.

Be still and rest in Jesus. He is our rock. Stand strong in Jesus. Our Daddy, our Heavenly Father gives us the strength to press forward. He is the one to run to when we are weak. God is our security and protection. He shields us from the wicked fiery darts. God has given us the power and authority to cast down every demonic force. We are to tread upon serpents and take over authority over the Devil. God has given us the authority and dominion over the earth. When we get in God's presence, then we become the light of the world and the salt of the earth. Our Daddy helps us in the midst of storms and delivers out of bondage. We have to surrender ourselves to Jesus to be his instrument. God wants us to open our hearts to Jesus, so that he can work his power through us. He has given us everything we need to enhance and build the kingdom, but we have to know who he is. Also, we have to know who we are in Christ.

Do you fully trust God to handle your finances, relationships, business, or marriage? When we know who God is, then we don't have to worry about anything. You might be thinking, "How do I do that? I have to pay my bills and my marriage is falling apart." I want to ask you "Have you given it to God? When are you going to let go of the cares of the world? How are you going to fix it?" God tests us to see if we fully trust him. A year ago, I decided that only God can change people and he is the only one who can do the impossible. You really have to stop and ask yourself, "Do I try to figure it out or do I hand it over to God?" Your response determines the results you will receive. What you are willing to walk away from will determine what God will bring to you. Put your confidence and trust in God. In Proverbs 3:5, "Trust in the Lord with all of thine heart and lean not unto thine own understanding." We have to stop trying to make everything work out, and just trust our Father. He doesn't want us to trust our own understanding. God wants us to go to him and ask for wisdom and knowledge. He knows what we need. Ask and you shall receive. When we trust him, then he puts his angels to work. He guards us and protects us with his heavenly angels to carry out his plan. Dwell in the secret place with him and he will help you towards living a victorious life.

God can only do what we let him. He will not force his love upon us. We have to allow him to enter in and use us to be a blessing to others. He has equipped and prepared us to be warriors in his kingdom, but we have to spend time in his word. God wants us to meditate on his word and speak it in into existence. We are to memorize his word and act on it by faith. God desires for us to spend time in prayer and be ready for battle when we go into the world. When we are under the shadow of the Almighty, then we have his power and strength to take on anything and everything he instructs us to fulfill. Be obedient and of good courage. Know God is on your side and he is fighting your battles for you. Trust in your Heavenly

Father and you will see his goodness working in your life. Jesus loves you and God loves you. Be Blessed.

Gratitudes

†

"In all thy ways acknowledge him, and he shall direct thy paths."
Proverbs 3:6

First of all, I thank our Heavenly Father for his precious Son, Jesus Christ. When I was 18 years old, I was broken, hurt, abused, emotional, and lost, but Jesus pulled me out of the pit of hell. Jesus used mighty women and men of God to reach and pull me out with his love, hope, and joy. The darkest day of my life is when I received light. The light is Jesus Christ. I opened my heart and accepted Jesus Christ as my Lord and Savior. I thank God that there are people on earth being used as a vessel for the kingdom of heaven. Now, God is using me as a vessel to inspire and encourage others through my testimony to come to Jesus Christ.

By writing this book, God gave me a whole new perspective in his purpose for my life. He gave me insight in how he used his people to lead me straight to the source – Jesus Christ. Through these powerful men and women of God, I learned not only to be a giver but to be a receiver. God answered my prayers by surrounding me with wise counsel and individuals that never gave up on me or loved me for who I am in Christ Jesus.

The following people are leaders, mentors, teachers, and encouragers who have left footprints of hope, love, joy, patience, victory, or beauty on the surface of my heart: Leah Coleman, Cheryl Jarvis, Rachel Loughlin, Rhonda Redman, Pat

Thompson, Ginger Weeden, Tania Banks, Ashley Duke, Patricia Branch, Dorcas

Garner, Gail Farrell, Andrew Harrison, Lindsay May Robinson, Charles George,

James Holland, Etti Baranoff, Sidney Bostian, Bridget Grindstaff, Micah Winn,

Michelle Boswell, Melissa Miller, Dorcas Garner, Cherie Tew, Nadine Williams,

Hadassah Carter, Linda Pegram, Angelia Shay, Dad and of course, my amazing

husband, Kyle Moore. I give God all of the glory for using all of you in my life and

thank you for having the willingness to be used for his kingdom. Your friendship,

partnership, relationship, or mentorship encouraged and helped me to identify

God's purpose and plan for my life. Your dedication and commitment to help

God's people is glorifying his kingdom. I encourage you to continue being the

light in your home, workplace, business, or wherever God has placed you to be a

blessing.

About the Author

†

"Trust in the Lord with all thine heart; lean not unto thine own understanding."

Proverbs 3:5

Megan M. Moore grew up in a broken childhood filled with abuse, rejection, fear, and abandonment. Her faith in Jesus Christ has brought her out of the darkness and into a life of deliverance, healing, and joy. Megan's message of more than an over comer and healing has touched lives of hundreds of women across Virginia.

Megan M. Moore is a member of Faith Landmarks Ministerial Fellowship and actively serves at Faith Landmarks Ministries. She is a follower of Jesus Christ, leader, more than an overcomer, and uplifting motivational speaker and author. Megan is happily married and deeply devoted to her husband, Kyle, who is a constant source of love and encouragement to her. They make their home in Saint Stephens Church, Virginia with their dog, Wilbur Cletus Moore. You can visit her blog at womenconnectwomenministry. wordpress.com or facebook at KyleMegan Moore Wcwm or email at womenconnectwomenministry@yahoo.com.

THE

HISTORY AND CONVERSION

OF

SAMUEL HARRIS,

A POLISH JEW,

CONTAINING AN ACCOUNT OF HIS EARLY LIFE, OF HIS TRAVELS, WHICH COMMENCED IN HIS FOURTEENTH YEAR, AND OF THE MANNER IN WHICH HE WAS LED TO EMBRACE

THE CHRISTIAN FAITH,

In the Year 1826, when he was

BAPTISED BY THE REV. W. CLEGG,

In Pitt-Street Chapel, Liverpool;

INTERSPERSED WITH ILLUSTRATIONS OF

Jewish Opinions, Customs & Expectations.

WRITTEN BY HIMSELF.

———

"But this I confess unto thee, that after the way which they call heresy, so worship I the God of my fathers, believing all things that are written in the law and the prophets." Acts xxiii. 16.

———

BRADFORD:

PRINTED FOR AND SOLD BY THE AUTHOR.

Price One Shilling.

1833.

Entered at Stationers' Hall.

H. WARDMAN, PRINTER, BRADFORD.